FIRM
FOUNDATION

Resilience AFTER TRAUMA

by

BONNIE SHUE MCDONALD

Published by hope*books
2217 Matthews Township Pkwy
Suite D302
Matthews, NC 28105
www.hopebooks.com

hope*books is a division of hope*media

Printed in the United States of America

First edition.
Paperback ISBN: 979-8-89185-409-3
Hardcover ISBN: 979-8-89185-354-6
Ebook ISBN: 979-8-89185-355-3
Library of Congress Number: Request Submitted

Endorsements

As a therapist who works extensively with trauma, grief, and relational challenges, I found *Firm Foundation: Resilience After Trauma* to be a profoundly practical and spiritually insightful guide for navigating life's storms. The book's metaphors of building and restoration resonate deeply, offering readers tangible ways to process pain, practice gratitude, and embrace God's redemptive work. I appreciate how it combines faith-based wisdom with actionable steps that foster healing, resilience, and hope. This is a great resource for anyone seeking to heal from even the most difficult life circumstances through God's loving guidance and the support of deep relationships.

—Monica L. Mouer, MS, LCMHCS, CSAT-S,
Certified EMDR Therapist

Bonnie Shue McDonald's book is more than a personal testimony of triumph over trauma. It is filled with practical suggestions about how we can face and respond to the inevitable setbacks and losses in our lives. I personally appreciate the study format, complete with questions and exercises to make immediate application of the principles of the book, while reflecting prayerfully on our real hope in Jesus Christ towards healing and restoration. Highly recommend!

—Suzy McCall, Missionary and Founder of
The LAMB Institute, Tegucigalpa, Honduras

Firm Foundation: Resilience After Trauma is a powerful guide for anyone navigating past trauma. Bonnie uses clear, practical steps and the vivid imagery of a home to help readers process hard experiences without feeling overwhelmed. Her thoughtful approach leads you toward understanding and hope, making space for healing in a safe and steady way. Whether you're working through your own story or supporting someone you love, this book is an invaluable resource. I highly recommend it.

—Catherine Honeycutt, President + CEO,
Honeycutt Media

I had the privilege of walking alongside Bonnie and her family during the intense times as a close friend to her son, and here is what I know about Bonnie: she walks in faith in every circumstance, and she has done so in the highs and lows. So, if you need some encouragement in your healing journey, she is gifted and graced to give you just that through *Firm Foundation: Resilience After Trauma*. You won't regret it, because you'll see a transformation in yourself.

—Harrison Skey, Senior Manager of Spanish Internet Evangelism,
Billy Graham Evangelical Association

Dedication

To my dear mother,
Mary Eyvonne Barringer Shue

Thank you for showing me what it means to know the Lord through your godly life and the way you've reflected Jesus in everyday moments.

May countless others be drawn to Him because of your faithful example.

Acknowledgments

This book would not be possible without the many resources and education provided to me through hope*books. It was through this publisher that I met my writing coach and formed meaningful friendships with others who encouraged me and generously shared their knowledge and experience, helping bring this book to life.

Many thanks to Stephanie Miller, my writing coach, who prayed with me and spent countless hours guiding me along the writing path.

Thank you to my husband, Flint, who said, *"Yes, do it."* He encouraged me and never once complained about the time required to complete this work, so that I might be obedient to God's direction. Thank you to my children for their loving support. I love all of you!

Recipe for Sundrop Pound Cake

3 cups plain flour

3 cups sugar

5 eggs

½ cup butter flavored Crisco

2 sticks room temperature butter (not margarine)

1 tsp. Lemon flavoring

1 tsp. Vanilla flavoring

6 oz. Sundrop (or any citrus soda)

Mix in the order listed. Bake at 325° F for 1 hour and 15 minutes.

Recipe by Amy Schueneman (used with permission)

Table of Contents

Letter to Reader

Dear Reader,

Can I share something with you? I never set out to write this book. In fact, if you had asked me before 2013, I would have told you I wasn't sure I had words for a book. But sometimes life delivers a story that shows us that the only way through it is to write.

This book was born out of a hard season or two that stretched me, threatened to break me, and ultimately reshaped me. Through it all, I knew the Lord was the One keeping me going. And somewhere in the middle of the ache, I felt Him nudging me to put pen to paper. At first, I wasn't sure if the writing was for me, to help me process the pain, or for you, the one who might need to know you're not alone. Maybe it's both.

My struggle came from medical situations that faced my immediate family members. Life-adjusting diagnoses and consequences that don't allow for any lifestyle improvements in order to get better. Our world and people around us have a hard time accepting that there are diagnoses without solutions. That didn't make anything easier and many had a "did you try…?" solution. I am the helper in the story. The mother, the wife. The one trying to hold things together in everyday life (medical provider paths, appointments, and all the related communication), and being held together by the only One who can actually do that.

I don't know your story, but I know what it feels like to walk through something that changes everything. If you're reading this right now, I imagine you do too. Our hard stories may not look the same, but I believe they intersect in the deep places—where pain meets purpose, where loss meets hope, and healing that always begins in the hands of our Creator.

More than anything, I want you to hear this:

You are not alone.

The weight you carry matters.

And so does the person you are becoming because of it.

Some see trauma only as a horrible thing that has been endured. Those who experience "little trauma" over years are also enduring trauma. It may not be *horrible* when compared to the plight of those who have survived "big trauma" like human trafficking, wrongful imprisonments, kidnapping, and other atrocities; however, all can benefit from healing. Healing helps trauma of every size. All trauma is experienced from a personal perspective so all are valid, free from comparison.

If these pages can offer His light in your darkness, then every word is worth writing.

Thank you for allowing me to walk a little bit of your journey with you.

In a spirit of hope,
Bonnie Shue McDonald

Introduction

Where does one begin with a large project? With the foundation.

My husband has spent his life building homes, so I know more than most about the importance of a strong foundation. I've seen how weather, materials, and craftsmanship influence not only the structure itself but its longevity for future generations. As a residential realtor, I've also learned to notice the quiet signs of wear, the impact of storms over time, and the strength or weakness of what lies beneath the surface.

The same is true for the foundation of our lives—and for this book.

One winter morning, my longtime friend and prayer partner, Dianne, and I were walking along the beach, admiring the oceanfront homes. We found ourselves commenting on their features. Some had protective shutters, others with upper-level pools, some clearly weathered by salty air and storm-driven waters. After we talked, a scripture came to mind:

> Unless the LORD builds the house, those
> who build it labor in vain.
> Psalm 127:1

Later that morning, I sat down and wrote. The images from our walk—the homes, their vulnerability, the wisdom of their construction—began to blend with the metaphor of life. If God is the builder, and our lives are the house, then the strength of what we're building depends entirely on who is leading the work.

A builder doesn't guess; he follows time-tested practices passed down through generations. In the same way, we're called to prepare our hearts, using the truth of God's Word, our unshakable foundation.

Storms will come. A wise builder watches the weather, understands how water moves across the land, and positions the home to withstand oncoming danger. Oversight is constant. Quick attention to vulnerable areas can prevent deeper damage. And when storms do hit, the size and speed may not be within our control, but our response always matters.

What methods are most effective for helping the home to thrive for generations—built for longevity, not for a short-term gain? Who needs to be engaged to make the most of each aspect of the home? The builder oversees it all, but also uses the gifts and talents of others to carry out the whole project … our whole lives.

Anticipating next steps is a key to managing expectations. The builder knows the existing home will face challenges that will be uncovered in the renovation and repair process. The old must be considered for adherence to the new. What needs to be torn out and replaced altogether and what can be utilized for the future? What experts will aid in the process? And what on-going processes will allow the home to be a thriving shelter for generations? The builder knows that a poorly maintained home is at risk for greater damages. He desires the work of his hands to thrive and helps it to do so through the storms of life.

I've found that using a home as a metaphor for healing makes the process feel more tangible, less overwhelming, and even less emotionally charged… to help us steward our emotions well. When we picture our healing as the careful construction of a home, one layer at a time, with intentional preparation, we remove some of the fear and pressure.

Healing is not fast.

It takes time.

It takes grace.

And it takes the wisdom of our Creator, the Master Builder.

I am eternally grateful for those who planted seeds of faith in my life, leading me to know Jesus. Faith in Christ isn't a one-time decision; it's a foundation that must be strengthened, cultivated, and built upon. While many people struggle with their faith in times of trouble, through every trial I have faced, my faith has been a stabilizing force. Time and again, I've found myself whispering, *I don't know how people survive hardships without Him.* He is our Sustainer.

As we begin this journey together, you'll notice the chapters are short. That's intentional. When I was searching for books on trauma, I found some were too clinical and others too heavy to get through. Pain can make it hard to concentrate, to absorb, even to breathe. When we're in survival mode, small doses of truth and hope are often all we can manage.

So go gently. This isn't a race.

I wish I could sit with you over a cup of coffee and hear your story.

Your pain is valid. Your journey is unique.

This isn't a quick process. It's sacred ground.

Be kind to yourself. Progress—no matter how small—is worth celebrating. Healing isn't about perfection; it's about restoration. And restoration takes time.

So here we are, standing on the land that is your life. Before we build, we must prepare.

Grab a pen to write directly in the space provided.

Most importantly, let's begin with prayer.

A Prayer for the Journey

Lord, thank You for being our God. Thank You for bringing us to this moment with You. Guide us into all wisdom and understanding as we seek to know You more.

Prepare our hearts, Lord. Show us what needs tending, what needs confessing, and what needs surrendering. Give us courage to face our pain today and in the coming days rather than bury it, knowing that what remains hidden may trip us, or those we love, tomorrow.

Provide the right tools, wise counselors, and a circle of support to walk with us. Teach us patience, so we do not rush what You are carefully unfolding. Layer by layer, build our lives upon You—the only firm foundation. You know our hearts, Lord. If anything in us is not of You, bring it to light so we may lay it at Your feet. Lead us in Your way everlasting. In Jesus' name, Amen.

PART I

Naming What Hurts—Understanding the Wound

1

Help In the Moment

Trauma creates change you don't choose.
Healing is about creating change you do choose.[1]
Michelle Rosenthal

When a storm is over, the truth of what needs tending becomes clear. The devastation of a home, and the awareness that a storm has swept through the surrounding area, can shake anyone to the core.

You may find yourself recalling storms of your own. For that reason, imagine a house unfamiliar to you, perhaps like the one on the book cover, standing after the winds have passed. Picture it weathering the storm's force. The first glimpse of such a scene, and the losses it represents, can stir deep and challenging emotions.

The purpose of this anchoring paragraph about a house in each chapter is to give you a safe place to come back to as you

---

1 Rosenthal, Michelle. *Your Life After Trauma: Powerful Practices to Reclaim Your Identity.* My Trauma Coach, 13 May 2019, https://www. mytraumacoach.com/post/your-life-after-trauma-excerpt.

read. I have chosen to leave out the vivid details of my story so that you can continue reading without wearing out your emotions. This book can only encourage your healing if you are able to keep reading it, even when the subject is tender.

Picture the home as if you saw it on the news—someone else's story—and allow your feelings of compassion for those who live there to flow. Perhaps you whisper a prayer for their safety and provision, noticing the damage and the work ahead without being overwhelmed by it.

Return to this viewpoint whenever the content feels heavy, remembering that "God is our refuge and strength, a very present help in trouble" (Psalm 46:1).

On this first mental visit to the anchor home, you may choose not to step inside—there could be unseen damage, and entering too soon might not be safe. In the same way, I want to speak candidly with you: If reading these pages stirs significant anxiety, consider pausing, and seek wise counsel before continuing. Pausing doesn't mean failure; it means wisdom. Depending on your own story, it may be best to receive professional support before "going in." A helpful place for you to begin is Christian Care Connect in the Resource section of this book, where you can find trusted Christian therapists.

Being on the "other side" of healing doesn't mean that recalling the circumstances becomes easy. It is hard. I don't want to go there again in my mind. The reason I do is for you. The Lord has led me to share this story and I pray that my writing will honor His purposes.

My Story

Our team was favored to win. Mt. Pleasant High School has a long history of strength in the sport of wrestling, and our son had come up in the ranks of training at a local "coach house" and was now wrestling as a freshman. The "away" match quickly ended with our team's win, but moments later, Matthew collapsed at the bench. We were in the stands and everything happened quickly. I flew down the bleachers to the gathering of people around him. I saw the physical abrasions, evidence of him hitting the floor. He was unconscious and making sounds I didn't want to hear. We didn't know it at the time, but he was in cardiac arrest. Lots of people, including the athletic trainer and coaches, were responding to the situation.

My own role was led by the Lord to pray. And I was PRAYING. Many prayerful words were spoken aloud as I prayed for God to put beats in Matthew's heart and blood to his brain. Repeatedly I prayed those words, thanking God for doing that very thing.

Everyone was told to leave the gym. As Matthew's fellow wrestlers scrambled out, some ended up outside near the parking lot, some in the locker room, and some in the hallway that connected to the school. Urgently, I told those in the hallway to pray and get everyone they knew to pray.

Around that same time, a parent of one of our wrestlers who happened to be a cardiac emergency room nurse, Sheri, arrived a little late to the match. She knew our team was favored to win. She also knew the match was likely already over, *but for some reason* she decided to come into the gym anyway. We know the *reason*. God was directing her steps.

She quickly assessed what was happening and jumped in to lead the charge on compressions. In the chaos, God had already placed two additional helpers. They had come forward from the crowd to help. A former EMS worker. The parent of the student athletic trainer. These two people were also our friends. *They were responding to Matthew's needs*. The original

AED provided by the school did not have the appropriate parts. So the three angels in action took turns with compressions.

Sheri came over to me and asked me to come and put my hands on Matthew. I thought she was asking me to do that because he wasn't going to make it. When I put my hand on him, the other hand reached to the heavens and the words of a hymn flowed from my mouth as loud as I could sing:

> All hail the power of Jesus' name!
> Let angels prostrate fall.
> Bring forth the royal diadem,
> and crown him Lord of all.
> Bring forth the royal diadem,
> and crown him Lord of all![2]

The EMS arrived and took over with their own AED that would then be used to cardiovert his heart three times before he was stable for transportation. From there, the details are blurry. I felt the Holy Spirit carrying me.

Earlier that very morning, my Bible reading had been from John 14:15–31. Only later did I realize that God used this scripture to guide me in the circumstances as they occurred. He prepared me through the morning's reading.

> But the helper, the Holy Spirit, whom the Father will send
> in my name, he will teach you all things and bring
> to your remembrance all that I have said to you.
> John 14:26

---

2 Perronet, Edward. *All Hail the Power of Jesus' Name, 1779. Hymns and Psalms*, Public Domain.

I usually choose one verse in particular to journal with reflection. I had written about the Holy Spirit and my gratitude for the knowledge that I have a helper with me all the time. The Holy Spirit guided me in prayer in the presence of many witnesses. He helped me and others to pray for Matthew in the exact moments that he needed it.

My husband, Flint, was on the floor beside Matthew, encouraging him to hang on and not give up. My role was continually clear—pray. I was pacing *in another place spiritually*, praying aloud with all the urgency of a mother calling on her Lord.

Not my will, but yours, be done.
Luke 22:42b

On the way to the Monroe hospital, I called two friends and had to leave urgent messages for them to pray. I also posted on Facebook: "Your will, not mine. Pray for Matthew McDonald now." Minutes later, I filled the emergency room with my loud prayerful pleas for everyone to hear. The life-flight team surrounded Matthew and I heard words come from his mouth: "My feet are cold." Praise God from whom all blessings flow. I am filled with tears all over again as I celebrate this miracle.

We knew he was stabilizing. He could form a sentence! He had blood in his brain and beats in his heart.—answers to my prayers. Before he uttered those words, he was set to be transferred to Charlotte via life flight. Once he talked and, I am sure, passed other medical markers, the flight wasn't needed and he was transferred by ambulance instead. The amount of relief we felt was incomprehensible.

Later that night, the cardiac ICU medical team at Levine Children's Hospital in Charlotte celebrated with us. The compressions saved our son's life. Their words were, "Where is the miracle boy from Mt. Pleasant?" We praise God not only for sparing Matthew's life but for reminding us that even in crisis, He surrounds us with people prepared to help. They faithfully used their gifts in the setting they found themselves that night.

When Flint and I made our way to the hospital, we were lost. Matthew was no longer in the emergency department. Finally, we were told to go around to the front of the hospital. We had to be checked in with photo identification and everything took forever. (If you have an emergency, one parent should stay with the child, but we were not thinking clearly.)

The first thing I did was go over to him for a hug and I whispered in his ear, "You know it is a miracle that you are alive, don't you?" Since he had been unconscious, he had no recollection of any of the events. Praise God for His mercy in this regard. Flint and I were flooded with gratitude for so many things at once. Clearly we were celebrating his life and the life-giving measures that saved him. We were equally thrilled that our son already knew salvation through Jesus Christ before this happened. Not only because Matthew would have gone to heaven if God chose that, but because he had the firm foundation in Christ to help him navigate the challenging road ahead.

The Holy Spirit is my Helper—not only in emergencies but in all of life. In the gymnasium that evening, I had control over only one thing—the intention and urgency to pray. The Holy Spirit interceded and guided my prayers. He guided me to communicate to get others to pray, which was comforting to me.

We were able to clearly see evidence of God having laid groundwork for us: salvation, precise scripture, people who pray, and people present with the right skills. Our continual surrender to God not only lets us live spiritually free each day, but it allows a path for our surrendered lives to become whole regardless of our physical circumstances.

When we live in a posture of continual surrender, we make space for God's strength to meet us in our weakness. The Spirit is not limited to moments of crisis. Jesus promised that He would teach us all things and remind us of His words in every circumstance. That means surrender isn't just for when our world collapses—it's something we practice daily, in the small decisions and the ordinary moments. Even years later, trauma leaves a trail and we will continually submit those consequences to the Lord. The same Spirit who carried us through a life-and-death moment longs to carry you through today's uncertainties too.

When the winds of the storm are finally quiet, the house still stands—but its foundation tells the story. That night in the hospital, I saw our own foundation holding firm. The same is true for you: whatever storm has hit, your foundation in Christ can be strengthened as you begin to rebuild.

Have you named the storm that has tried or is trying to take you down? Are you lying in the midst of remnants just realizing what has happened? Not everyone has a storm that is over in a short amount of time. Maybe yours has endured for decades. The Lord knows all things and He knows His intentions for your release of all circumstances to Him. He doesn't expect us to handle this on our own, and He makes a way from the ground up so that your life can be restored just like the physical structure of a home. He desires redemption for you. In the early days of our storm, a worship song, "I Am" by Crowder, filled my heart with peace. You can find it in the Resources. I hope you find it equally peaceful.

From a biblical perspective, surrender is the choice to voluntarily submit all personal desires, will, and control to the lordship of Jesus Christ. God demands *total* surrender. Hang on to Him alone. We submit ourselves completely to Him as Romans 12 describes:

> I appeal to you therefore, brothers, by the mercies of God,
> to present your bodies as a living sacrifice,
> holy and acceptable to God,
> which is your spiritual worship.
> Do not be conformed to this world,
> but be transformed by the renewal of your mind,
> that by testing
> you may discern what is the will of God,
> what is good and acceptable and perfect.
> Romans 12:1–2

Reflection Questions

1. What is one thing you are holding tightly that you can release to the Lord today?

2. What are your current practices for surrendering to God daily?

3. What helps you remain in a surrendered posture through-
    out the day?

4. Where have you seen God's faithfulness in the past that
    encourages you to release everything again now?

Daily Practice

I am so grateful I had established the practice of seeking God
daily and that I did it *that day*! It is one of the reasons I never
want to miss my time alone with God because I know He is
equipping me for the specific day that I am about to live. I
don't want to miss the ways in which He is preparing me. Set
aside time daily to be in His presence, even if you begin with
five minutes. Connection with Him is the goal.

Your Turn

Have you surrendered your life to the Lord and received the
gift of salvation? We would all miss the whole point of this
book entirely without the plan for salvation. The message of
the Gospel has been clearly presented in resources like *Steps to
Peace With God*, which outlines the journey to reconciliation
with God.[3] If you already know Jesus as your Savior, this is a
great time to practice sharing His message:

---

3 Adapted from *"Steps to Peace With God."* PeaceWithGod.net, Billy
  Graham Evangelistic Association, https://peacewithgod.net/steps/.

1. God loves us and wants us to experience His peace and life (see John 3:16).
2. Being at peace with God is not automatic, because by nature we are separated from God because of sin (see Romans 3:23).
3. When Jesus Christ died on the cross and rose from the grave, He paid the penalty for our sins (see 1 Peter 2:24).
4. God gives us the right to become children of God when we believe in Him (see John 1:12).
5. We simply pray to God that we admit our sin. We repent and are willing to turn from that sin. We believe Jesus Christ died on the cross and was raised from the dead. We receive Him as our personal Lord and Savior.

Whether you're surrendering to Christ for the first time or returning again, each act of yielding opens space for healing.

By telling the Lord of our dependence on Him, seeking His Word and actively living it out, we are able to know that He will prepare each of us for our activated assignments daily. Write out the answers to the reflection questions. If that is too much, begin with the Pause App (see Resources) and listen in for ways that help you surrender control of all of your life.

Prayer

Lord, I praise You for being a faithful God and equipping me for each moment You allow. Forgive me for the times I have not been faithful and have not come to You in surrender. Thank You for accepting me just as I am. Thank You for extending forgiveness to me over and over. Thank You for allowing me to be reading this book and learning ways that will improve my relationship with You and my life so that I can lean into all You have planned for me. Help me, Lord, to stick with it. Teach me to keep surrendering what I cannot control, trusting that You will bring beauty from the broken pieces. Help me to embrace what is needed and to bring glory to Your name because of it. In Jesus' name I pray. Amen.

2

The Truth About Trauma

*You may not control all the events that happen to you,
but you can decide not to be reduced by them.*[4]
Maya Angelou

Let's take the needed time to assess the damage of the home after the storm, making notes of the needs. If the kitchen has been damaged and you are still able to live in the house even after "normal routine" settles back in, adjustments must be made. Finding a new space for preparing meals is necessary, like moving the microwave and the coffee pot to an accessible place for continued use while renovations occur. You are setting up alternative "housekeeping," but the damage of the home needs to be assessed.

The great difference between home damage and personal trauma is that a home can be rebuilt by other workers. Personal trauma must be tackled by YOU. You cannot delegate this work to someone else. If you don't do it, it won't get done. Yes,

---

4 Angelou, Maya. *Letter to My Daughter*. Random House, 2008.

other helpers or workers are often required, but you are the lead person to get the repair started.

Repairs cannot begin without an assessment. Which of your senses are affected by the damages in this house? What is seen physically? Is there a smell of something unseen, like mildew or mold? Do you hear anything? Are certain parts of the house volatile to touch? A system for handling the situation must be put into place.

The Jethro Principle in Action

An incident that occurred a few years ago came to mind and made me grateful for support systems that were already in place. I was the Youth Director at my church for fifteen years. I had a CDL license and drove the students to and from all of the ministry events. We were coming down the mountain of I-40E from Asheville toward McDowell County in North Carolina. We had just spent a week at Snowbird Wilderness Outfitters Mission Camp and the students were hyped to be concluding a great week, testifying about all they had seen and heard.

We had a rocking playlist for the bus, so I turned it up and let them enjoy themselves. Meanwhile, I focused on the road, and one of the great men in our church, Jeremy Petrea, hung out with the students. I heard a loud pop and thought, *That's odd; I don't remember that in this song.* Jeremy and I realized that we just had a tire blow out on this 30-passenger bus while driving 55 mph down an interstate. We were located just past the McDowell County Rest Area. I slowed to a stop, turned on the flashers, and Jeremy directed our plan. He went to redirect traffic so that I could back the bus from the interstate onto the exit ramp of the rest area. We then called our church contact, John, who was in charge of our church buses, and he began the search for a tire service to come help us.

There were a lot of people at the rest area, as it had been discovered to be a Pokemon Go location (a cultural geocaching game at the time); and, of course, we were super protective of the students in our care. We waited for three hours for the tire service to arrive with our new tire, spending the time talking, reading, and playing cards. The students were amazing. We had notified their parents on the app we used for parent communication. They were patiently awaiting our return. (We arrived back at home four hours later than planned.)

The good news: There were lots of helpers. Jeremy was directing traffic and helping me keep the students safe. John was handling the search for the tire service. The tire service located the tire we needed. The student leaders kept the games, conversation, and book read-aloud going. I communicated with all the various resources and let the parents know about our updates and that all students were safe.

It was a hot July Saturday and we were at a *rest area* with lots of available drinks and snacks, bathrooms, picnic tables, and shelters to keep us cool. I hope you can see all of God's provision in this setting and the helpers. It all left me feeling tired, but oh so grateful. Things could have ended much worse.

This reminds me of a leadership lesson taught by our pastor: One person cannot do it all. The Jethro Principle (see Exodus 18:13–26) outlines the manner of appointing capable trustworthy leaders to oversee particular tasks. Moses was experiencing a challenge managing the requests of those coming to him in order to know God's will. Jethro recognized the problem and told Moses not to wear himself out meeting with every person. "What you are doing is not good" (Exodus 18:17b). He directs Moses to select men who are capable,

God-fearing, trustworthy, and honest and appoint them to do the duties needed. Essentially, Jethro is telling Moses to develop a system.

> What you are doing is not good. You and the people
> with you will certainly wear yourselves out, for the
> thing is too heavy for you. You are not able to do it alone.
> Exodus 18:17b–18

Jethro told Moses, and I am telling you. You need capable, God-fearing, trustworthy, and honest leaders of your choosing to help you navigate your own life. These people can come alongside you in the manner that you need, but other people need to be involved to help you learn what you *do not yet know* in order to heal.

When support systems are in place, it is easy to call upon your counselor and schedule a session, but maybe you don't already have a counselor. If you attend a church, your church may have a support system in place for counseling. Talk to your pastor for direction or seek out a trusted friend who has experienced a trauma.

Studies show that while *nearly everyone* experiences trauma, not everyone develops post-traumatic stress disorder (PTSD). In fact, only a minority—5.6 percent—go on to develop PTSD. Yet for those who do, the weight of it can be life-altering. Studies suggest that up to 40 percent of people with PTSD recover within the first year, but that still leaves many who continue to suffer for years without relief.[5]

---

5 "Post-Traumatic Stress Disorder." *World Health Organization*, 27 May 2024, https://www.who.int/news-room/fact-sheets/detail/post-traumatic-stress-disorder.

I am so grateful to be in the category who recovered from PTSD within the first year. The sobering reality is that we cannot predict who will experience PTSD and who will need more intentional counseling or longer duration of help to heal.

Part of recovery is developing our self-awareness. I quickly learned the importance of recognizing feeling unsafe. I noticed right away that I felt nauseated and anxious *at the thought* of returning to a high school gymnasium anywhere. Athletic fields, or really anything to do with high school athletics, brought about the same nausea—making me want to always know the location of the nearest bathroom.

As the parent of two high school athletes and the youth director who often watched our youth group students in their chosen sports, I knew I couldn't avoid these places. I forced myself to show up as part of my parenting and my role in the lives of those in our church family. Therefore, I reached out to a trusted friend who is also a counselor and briefly shared the circumstances. She recommended a Christian counselor who specializes in EMDR (Eye Movement Desensitization and Reprocessing) therapy. It involves three senses: sight, sound, and touch. The therapist activates your senses while talking you through the trauma that is affecting your life. That therapy enabled Flint and me to overcome the battle in our minds, anxiety, and the constant replay of the scenes we had witnessed.

Help from counselors, faith communities, or trusted guides is essential. Trauma statistics are not meant to discourage but to remind us that needing help is normal, common, and human. We encounter small traumas and large traumas in our lives. Some people even refer to traumas as "little t" or "big T." Each depends on the perspective of the individual. No matter the degree of the trauma, healing is possible through the right support systems. We are not created to walk this road alone.

An assessment of our needs by someone else can feel heavy, but it serves a purpose—just like a home inspection after a storm. The assessor helps us see what's really there so we can rebuild with intention. As you move into the reflection questions, think of this as a time to identify which areas of your "house" need tending right now and which can wait for another season.

Reflection Questions

1. What are the thoughts, feelings, behaviors, or emotions that come up repeatedly in your life? Writing these down can grow your self-awareness.

2. Do you tend to minimize your own trauma by comparing it to others, or can you see your pain as valid?

3. Who has God already placed in your life that you can lean on for support right now?

Daily Practice

- Name One Burden: Write down one area where you've tried to "carry it all" alone. Pray about who might help you share that load.

- Identify Your Circle: List 2–3 safe, trusted people who can walk with you in your healing.

- Ground in Scripture: Write Exodus 18:18 or Psalm 46:1 on a card or post-it note and carry it with you or post it as a reminder you are not meant to walk alone.

Your Turn

Choose one practice today—whether naming a burden, identifying your circle, or grounding yourself in Scripture. Begin small, but take one step toward healing with support.

Prayer

Lord, thank You that I don't have to carry my burdens alone. Thank You for being the provider of helpers through the Holy Spirit, counselors, pastors, and friends to walk with me. Forgive me when I try to do it on my own or when I turn away from other help. Give me the courage to turn toward help and to reach for the support I need. Grant me the wisdom to recognize whom You've placed in my path. Remind me that healing is possible with You as my foundation. In Jesus' name, Amen.

3

Unresolved Past Trauma

If you continue to carry bricks from your past,
you will end up building the same house.
Unknown

Ever watched an episode of *This Old House*? We see the life of a home, and each homeowner leaves an impact. The manner in which they cared for the home shows up. For example, one owner may choose custom-made cabinets to match existing cabinetry. Another homeowner may choose a modern shower that best suits their physical needs, even though the modern finishes don't match the era of the home. Each owner's way of doing things affects every future owner.

The project manager of the renovation will try to piece together history. How old is the house? What storms has it survived? The history may reveal repairs that have been made and how they have been made. Were permits obtained from the local inspector's office? Was the work done by experienced professionals or a do-it-yourself novice? With the answers to these details, the project manager can then help the owner decide which things might need full replacement or determine the aspects of the house that can remain in place. For the work practices that have been greatly improved, replacement can be considered counting the financial cost and time that will affect the completion of the whole project.

In the same way, when we begin healing from trauma, we may need to re-evaluate areas of our life that were patched up too quickly or never properly repaired at all. That close examination can reveal emotional damage we didn't realize was still affecting us or our relationships with others. Pain may be "covered over" so to speak.

Family of Origin

Only after close examination in my healing process did I realize that my angry outbursts are usually in response to someone imposing demands onto me. Therapy helped me recognize that my dad's demanding nature and my response to it needed to be addressed.

Dad was a sergeant in the army, and often I felt like we were in-house soldiers who received doled-out demands that were harsh and unreasonable. Some of these were: Don't come to the table for breakfast unless you are dressed (no pajamas allowed), face washed, hair and teeth brushed. And, you had to be present immediately when you were called! "Yes, sir, here I am, reporting for breakfast." I never said that aloud, but the sarcasm inside of me was surely thinking about it. To say that would have been an affront to him, and the punishment would have been harsh and unreasonable. Miss your 10:30 p.m. curfew by 10 minutes? You were grounded "until I say so." Looking back, I can see that his structure came from a place of control, not care. I know that he did care sometimes; however, his version of the army left me walking on eggshells.

My husband will share that telling me how to drive elicits an angry outburst, especially if the traffic setting is intense. I have learned to level down in other settings, but in the tension of driving, I can still lose control. To work against that, I try to avoid certain driving patterns. I avoid driving at busy times of the day, being in a hurry in general, and dangerous intersections. The intensity is more likely to bring an outburst, so I intentionally avoid these things when possible. I also seek the Lord in helping me surrender these outbursts to Him. They have become less frequent, but the threat still exists within me. These are all things I only learned *after* this larger trauma occurred.

Your view of fractured relationships may gain a new perspective. The strained relationship between my dad and *his* mother caused me and my siblings to not have a relationship with her at all. That could have been for our best interest. My mom shared in recent years that my paternal grandmother was the meanest person she had ever met. My mother hardly ever speaks that way about anyone. I knew it must have been bad. Whatever traumas were experienced by my paternal grandmother were unresolved, and that affected all of her children and grandchildren: part of the cost of not healing.

Perhaps some traumas that come into awareness simply need acknowledgement. An ah-ha moment that brings greater understanding. There may also be experiences that you have not recognized previously as a problem... and suddenly they are understood as a problem that needs to be addressed. Did something happen in your past and you have just accepted it as part of your life? Now, with an additional layer of trauma, these can be revealed as a battle you didn't realize you have been fighting. Just as an old house holds evidence of every hand that's worked on it, our lives carry the marks of those who came before us. Are you considering those from your own family of origin?

The marks in all of our lives are evidence of our upbringing. I had a lot of reasons to respect my dad: He had natural leadership, an entrepreneurial spirit, and a good work ethic. He was attentive to details and would always "tell it like it is." He even planned his own funeral. That might be morbid to some, but it helped us so much when he passed that I immediately followed his example and took care of my own funeral preplanning.

Dad's sense of humor would either make you die laughing or die of embarrassment. I recall on many occasions that my mom was the subject of his "picking." And if she was not, someone else would be. He told many embarrassing stories over and over and usually in the presence of the one that it would embarrass. Now I wonder if Dad used humor as a coping mechanism for all the unspoken realities in his life—things he never addressed in healthier ways. Maybe he simply didn't know better. But we do. With access to healthier tools and greater awareness, we're responsible for using them. Our families of origin may not have known how, but we have the opportunity to do better—so let's choose to.

I have said for the last two decades that he taught me to be generous and he taught me to forgive, among other things. The generosity came naturally to him and I witnessed him give to others freely, especially someone who was down on their luck as he would call it. He was the first to respond when friends or family members would experience a devastating difficulty. I can only assume that his gifts to others were freely given. Most gifts to me came with a price: compliance with *all* of his preferences for an indefinite period of time… maybe forever. Let me explain.

When it was time to buy my first car, he went to the dealership while I was in class about to graduate from college. He later presented me with the payment book in my name (not sure how he pulled that off), and he picked the car. A brand new Ford Escort in the most plain model without even a radio. I did not have an ounce of input in purchasing my first new car that "I bought." That pattern, his control and my compliance (or rebellion against), showed up in many ways, both practical and emotional.

The verbal and emotional abuse that Dad dished out to me and my siblings could have taken me down, but something in me allowed me to forgive him over and over and move past the issue without reconciliation. He was the boss and we had to accept things as they were. He was not changing.

Having friends over was something I never considered. As a kid, I was afraid to have them visit my house because I never knew what might happen. How terrible it would be to accidentally make Dad angry, causing an outburst. The likelihood of this was great with my brothers in their teenage years and all of us moving in and about the house so often. Dad might throw things and would definitely throw plenty of harsh, degrading words. That was terribly embarrassing even in restaurants as an adult. So I never wanted to risk possible embarrassment in front of my friends. Or, even worse, embarrass my friend. I would much prefer to *leave* our house and go spend the night with a friend. The peace of a joyous family was so refreshing.

As an escape from dad and whomever he was "on the warpath" against, I remember reading books being my safe place. I would literally hide behind my bed with a book. In a home with five children, hiding was necessary to find privacy and avoid someone telling me a chore to do. I recall reading all of Carolyn Haywood's *Betsy* books, then later all of the Nancy

Drew collection. I have learned that reading is proven to be a stress reliever... no wonder I used it as a way to cope.

Somehow, getting lost in the story of *Little House on the Prairie* (I read all the Laura Ingalls Wilder books too) helped me forget about all the things happening around me. I could have my own private escape that brought some peace and joy. There have been seasons of not reading, but I find life to be more joyful when I have a good book in progress. Regardless of what happens in a day, the characters of the book are calling to me to come sit for a little bit, even if only for ten minutes. I still read every day now because I love it and it relieves stress. But thankfully, I don't have to hide it, and I have no need that requires escape.

Not everyone in my family remembers needing to find a way to escape. In conversations with at least two of my siblings, I have learned that one recalls experiences very similar to mine and one does not. At all. This has been demonstrated to me in real-life: Everyone receives and processes the past differently based on their own personality, experiences, perspective, and how the individual brain constructs and responds to reality.

Forgiving my dad daily is something I recall, but my siblings might tell a different story. I only know that I felt I *had to forgive him* in order to continually coexist in life in the same home. I continued to feel that way as an adult when I lived on my own. It is challenging when others recall a completely different set of circumstances. If your experience is not believed by others or remembered the same way that you do, it doesn't make it less real. Let's remind ourselves of that.

There are patterns that each of us lived in our childhood and then a pattern that you choose to embrace or move away from in adulthood. When a trauma occurs for a growth-minded person, the subsequent healing may introduce *yet another* pattern to one's life. When you choose to walk in the path of healing, the rewiring of your brain helps you in everyday recognition of what once seemed normal. Even now, revisiting those memories reminds me how easily unresolved pain and generational curses are disguised as "just the way things were."

We had been married only a few years when some friends came over to tell us they were getting a divorce. I had never known someone personally who divorced. Of course, the parents of some friends were divorced, but really that happened before I even had them as a friend. An "in progress" sort of thing was new to me. They explained that the husband had some situations that were holding them back. I perceive this unresolved issue as a consequence of trauma. After they left, I distinctly remember feeling disappointed for them as a couple and disappointed for their children's future. What were these "situations" holding them or him back? Couldn't they be resolved? Are your own situations coming to mind?

I have reflected on this point many times as a defining moment in my adulthood: If I am "adult enough" to realize a situation that needs attention, I am "adult enough" to do something about it. You are not required to extend acceptance because it is "just the way things are." We can choose to grow and do not have to settle into apathy. Apathy is defined as a behavior that shows no interest or energy and shows that someone is unwilling to take action, especially over something important.[6] In other words, if you want the grass to be greener, you better take the watering can with you.

---

6 "Apathy." *Cambridge Dictionary*, Cambridge University Press, https://dictionary.cambridge.org/us/dictionary/english/apathy.

Circumstances in my own life, including large and small traumas, have brought up reminders that I can choose to work through any unresolved trauma from the past or I can set a boundary if the other people do not want to work through the trauma. Healing people heal people (or help bring about healing). Hurting people hurt people. Essentially, we have two options:

1. To live in bondage to the trauma (past or current) we have endured and continually see ourselves as a victim.
2. To live in freedom from the trauma as we seek continual healing and see ourselves as captives set free to show others the way to freedom also.

It is a constant battle of the flesh and the Spirit to choose the bondage of the flesh or the freedom offered by the Spirit. The apostle Paul reminds us that this battle between old and new ways of living is not new—and we don't fight it alone.

> But I say, walk by the Spirit, and you will not gratify
> the desires of the flesh. For the desires of the flesh
> are against the Spirit, and the desires of the Spirit
> are against the flesh, for these are opposed to each
> other, to keep you from doing the things
> you want to do.
> Galatians 5:16–17

Every house renovation involves choices. Some pieces of the past can be restored, others must be replaced, and some need to be completely removed. We must be willing to truthfully assess the need.

Healing is the same. We can seek to restore relationships, but we can only do our part. The other party may be unwilling.

We can replace faulty thinking patterns with the renewing of our mind through the Word of God. We can remove ourselves from known situations likely to cause a major disruption. We can't rebuild on a faulty foundation. God invites us to partner with Him—the Master Builder—to decide what stays, what goes, and what can be made new.

Reflection Questions

1. What "old house" patterns from my past still show up in how I think or respond today?

2. Are there unresolved experiences I've minimized or dismissed that may still need care or attention?

3. Which parts of my past feel ready for repair, and which still feel too fragile to touch right now?

4. How does knowing the Spirit fights for my freedom bring comfort to me today?

Daily Practice

Take five minutes to journal today about a time when you felt your emotions stirred up, anxious, or unseen. Ask: *Is this connected to something old?* (Maybe a tone of voice, a rule, a fear of disappointing someone.) Write one sentence inviting God into that space: *Lord, show me how to rebuild this part of me with Your truth.*

Your Turn

Choose one small area where you sense God is asking you to release an old pattern or belief. Write it down, pray over it, and ask the Holy Spirit to help you respond differently the next time it arises. Healing is one decision of surrender at a time.

Prayer

Lord, thank You for being a God of freedom. Thank You for allowing me to know the truth and be set free by the truth of Your Word. Forgive me when I have turned away from Your Word and turned toward the world. Help me to continually turn toward You and Your ways. Help me to recognize when I'm rebuilding with old bricks from my past. Teach me to exchange them for Your materials of truth, grace, and freedom. Thank You for the power of the Holy Spirit who is helping me. Empower me to make the necessary choices at each moment of the day. You are God and I am not. Help me relinquish my rightful position each day. Allow me to live for Your glory alone. In Jesus' name I pray. Amen.

4

Overwhelmed

Trauma comes back as a reaction, not a memory.[7]
Bessel van der Kolk

Once the home's needs have been assessed, it's time to begin the repairs or renovations in the right order. As the list is made, priority is given to the specific circumstances. There is no need to measure, choose, or order replacement cabinetry when there are broken windows due to high winds. There is no need for new carpeting when the elements of weather are continually entering the home. There is an order to the project based on needs. Those needs and priorities will be assessed and reassessed as additional damages are uncovered. It is necessary to organize the workers so that too many people are not on the job and interfering with the progress of one another.

In the same way that order is needed in a home restoration, a daily path provides structure to each of us. Without a daily

---

7 Van der Kolk, Bessel. *The Body Keeps the Score: Brain, Mind, and Body in the Healing of Trauma.* Viking Press, 2014.

path, things can quickly become chaotic as our minds become disoriented and filled with apprehension rather than peace.

The brain, as affected by trauma, is like a house after a storm. There are many elements present (furnishings, wall hangings, decor, and personal items) and there are walkways evident from the arrangement of the home. The traumatic experience jumbles the brain as if someone picked up the house, gave it a big shake, and then set it down again. All the same contents are still there, but the walkways, also referred to as paths, that were once well-worn have been shaken about and are hard to find again. Because the brain is trying to find the old paths, repeating or returning to former routines is helpful. The introduction of new settings or circumstances can instantly bring a huge amount of overwhelm. Paths that were once known, but remain "out of order" can continue to overwhelm. In the setting of trauma, all of this is intensified. This is why everyday tasks can suddenly feel impossible—you're not broken; your brain is protecting you.

Joy That Overwhelms

My husband and I had been married for nine years before our first child and foolishly thought we had the parenting thing all set. We had read the books, bought the needed items, and made the plans. Our baby was due in June, and that date slightly interfered with our usual July 4th vacation week. "Oh, that's no big deal. We will go to the beach as usual, the guys will play golf, and I will rest in the house while all the girls are on the beach. (We vacationed with another family and their three adult daughters and spouses ... none of them had babies at the time.) The baby will just sleep most of the time anyway." Boy were we wrong.

I was nervous about everything. I was not sleeping well for fear that our baby would have a need and I would not know it. Each day, it seemed like an insurmountable challenge just to get a shower! Even though I had packed up all the new gadgets intended to help, I couldn't seem to get it altogether. I couldn't gather my thoughts or make any order for the day.

By day three, I had a little cabin fever from staying in the house so much. The beach was a few blocks away but felt like miles to me. Therefore, I had not even seen the ocean yet. Miriam, our little one, was only ten days old when we made the trip. She cried a lot. I cried a lot. And dear hubby was playing golf daily, so he didn't know the difference.

In the tradition of our community, everyone packs up and leaves our little town and many of us head to the same beach the week of the 4th of July. A family friend, Ms. Betty, came over to see Miriam and me at the beach house. I distinctly remember her saying, "We mamas have to stick together. I'll take the baby; you go take a shower. We will see the ocean after that." So I did as ordered. All the babies love Ms. Betty and I was not about to turn down a fresh pair of arms. We went to her oceanfront beach house, which provided a perfect view of the ocean without all the heat and direct sun.

By day five, Miriam had developed a cold and we packed up and headed home a little earlier than planned. We sat alongside the road multiple times to nurse her in the back seat of the car. What a long trip! Most certainly there was not a rested "vacation" feeling accompanying us on the way home.

This memory from 1996 brings back evidence of overwhelm. My new role as a mom included learning many new things I had not expected. I had new tools to use and had only been attempting to use those for ten short days. My body was making its own transition of needing physical rest and time to adjust emotionally with the changing hormones from childbirth. I was expecting too much of myself. Transporting our family and all of the gadgets along with our precious baby to the new setting of an unknown house was too much. Add a new bedroom set- up with a portable nursery, plus four sets of adults and no systems in place to help me navigate the way. This meant one overwhelmed version of me.

Take any new circumstance and transport it into a new setting and that gives opportunity for the overwhelm to multiply. In reflection, the wisdom the Lord has given me since then reminds me that going to the beach with a ten-day-old baby was not our best idea. Looking back, I see how that season taught me what overwhelm really feels like—and how God gives us wisdom as we reflect.

Recalling this memory not only reminded me of the overwhelm, but it reminded me of the amount of joy we had because we were so happy to finally be parents. There was much joy to be *able* to go on a beach vacation among treasured friends. When a memory comes to mind that has a happy time associated with it, our brain celebrates joy in the reflection. However, when memories come to mind that are associated with unhappy events and experiences, they remind our brain of the sadness of that event. It literally makes us feel sad all over again. Revisiting these thoughts in the disorganized state of a trauma-affected brain can feel like a flood, and that flood often contributes to the sense of overwhelm. The Lord desires for us to experience peace, not confusion. When I feel confused by the overwhelm, I remind myself of His truth:

> For God is not a God of confusion but of peace.
> 1 Corinthians 14:33

If sad memories are coming to your mind now and questions of "what if?" or "why didn't I?"— *pause. This is not a time to blame yourself for what you have endured.* Instead of allowing yourself to begin the questioning yet again, travel back to the thoughts of the house that is shaken up and out of order. Your mind wants a path that is clear and your questions make it unclear. Tell your mind to return again to think of the house repairs and order of priorities that are needed.

Just as a shaken house needs order and priorities to guide the repairs, our minds need the same clarity to avoid becoming overwhelmed. The following questions are meant to help you step back, notice what is really happening, and begin to sort through the chaos with gentleness. The mere act of reflection improves self-awareness and teaches the brain to notice details in the current moment.

Reflection Questions

1. Which thoughts or tasks keep circling in your mind and won't quiet down?

2. Which of these thoughts or tasks truly needs your attention now, and which can wait?

3. What physical signs (tight chest, foggy mind, restlessness) tell you that you're becoming overwhelmed?

4. When did you last notice yourself becoming suddenly overwhelmed? What was happening around you?

5. What simple routines or familiar paths (a walk, prayer, journaling, a safe place, a trusted person) help you feel more grounded?

Daily Practice (Multiple Options)

When the mental load grows and our thoughts spiral, we need a method to smooth things out. If you are in a difficult moment and need help while you are driving down the road, writing can't help then. A commonly known method to some is the 5, 4, 3, 2, 1 "grounding technique."

Counselors recommend it to redirect the mind by doing the following: Find five things you can see and name them. Find four things you can touch and name them. Find three things you can hear and name them. Find two things you can smell and name them. Find one thing you can taste and name it. If you are in a setting where naming them aloud is inappropriate, just name them in your mind. It helps to interrupt anxious thoughts and redirect your mind to your physical setting for a calm mindset. Your brain cannot maintain anxious thoughts and be in the present moment at the same time. It works!

Writing requires reflection and can clear a path forward and become a powerful tool for healing. Below are three methods for writing that can help you find your footing in the middle of the mess.

Read through all three to choose which suits you best at the moment. Just like a renovation site needs a project manager, your mind needs intentional guidance when circumstances become overwhelming. The act of writing helps you prioritize what matters today, sort through what can wait, and give you clarity when you are trying too much all at once. Whether it's a brain dump, a few free-flowing morning pages, or a clear grid of priorities, writing helps to create order in the mess.

- Brain dump: Write down every single thought that is coming to your mind. Write down every to-do, every sad thought, everything that you have been meaning to remind yourself or put on a calendar. Any groceries to buy or household items you need or forgot on your last trip. Who are you needing to make a return phone call to? Anything that comes to mind, write it down during the allotted time. Set a timer if that helps.

____

____

____

____

- Morning Pages: This is a journaling free-flow writing time. It also works best on a chosen time frame. Write your thoughts in sentences. It can be about anything. I often start by writing about the weather, a letter to God, or any other things that come into my mind. And if nothing comes to mind, I would write "nothing is coming to me at this moment" and keep writing that until other thoughts surface. Don't worry about grammar, spelling, or punctuation. Don't think about anyone else reading it. Just get it all down on paper to get it out of your head.

- Eisenhower Matrix[8]: This method helps when my thoughts need to be organized into priorities. It helps me tell my thoughts where to go, and I can categorize them based on urgency and importance on the matrix and then act on them accordingly. Use the blank diagram to fill in all your items.

	Urgent	Not Urgent
Important	DO	SCHEDULE
Not Important	DELETE	ELIMINATE

---

8 "The Eisenhower Matrix: Introduction & 3-Minute Video Tutorial." *Eisenhower.me*, FTL3, 2011–2025, https://www.eisenhower.me/eisen hower-matrix/.

Your Turn

Pick a method and spend at least ten minutes on that one method. The intention is to pick one based on your needs today rather than attempting all three.

We are not created to handle overwhelm on our own. The Lord desires for us to come to Him and surrender all of our joy and sorrow. He is Lord of all. Be authentic and transparent, allowing yourself to fully articulate to God all of your overwhelm. This is a healthy sign of our trust in Him.

Once we begin to put order to our overwhelm, it often becomes clear that wisdom from another person is necessary. Just as a house restoration requires many hands, our healing often requires trusted people to come alongside us. This is also explored in Chapter 2 and Chapter 9.

Prayer

Lord, I surrender all these thoughts to You. You are my God and the Creator of my mind. I surrender my mind, all my thoughts, and all that has been swirling in my mind as I read these pages. Forgive me for the times I have allowed the things of the world to capture my mind. Let me lay those down at Your feet. Help me as I read these pages to keep what is valuable and to discard what my mind is not able to process at this time. Thank You for Your sovereign plan in my life. Thank You for the moments I am able to read. Thank You for healing. Lord, heal my mind. Help me to trust You for order and know that chaos can be brought under Your control. Lord, grant me the wisdom in my life to know the path to pursue for healing. Help me to surrender all of this to You. Thank You, Lord. In Jesus' name I pray. Amen.

5

Faith Over Fear

The presence of fear does not mean you have no faith.
Fear visits everyone. But make your fear
a visitor and not a resident.[9]
Max Lucado

Most people think of a home as their safe place to be free to be themselves, to do as they wish, and to be protected from the outside world. Fears inside our home are usually related to the people in the home and their well-being. After the bigger things, like the foundation and load-bearing walls in a home renovation, where do the fears turn? It depends on the person and their experiences. Some will be concerned about what they cannot see (mold, moisture, electrical issues), safety features like railings, bannisters, properly operating doors, windows, an escape route in case of fire, smoke & carbon monoxide detectors. There are also the fears associated with keeping uninvited guests

---

9 Lucado, Max. *Live Loved: Experiencing God's Presence in Everyday Life.* Thomas Nelson Inc., 2011.

out. Eliminating entry points for pests and rodents, which are many times related to experiences. Fear can creep into our hearts the same way—through cracks we don't notice until we pause to inspect the foundation.

What hidden fears might still be living in your house, unnoticed but quietly influencing your peace?

Pandemic of 2020

Recalling the Pandemic in April 2020, I had built up this picture in my mind that once the Pandemic arrived in our town, it would sweep through like locusts or frogs referred to in the plagues that swept across Egypt. Everything would be wiped out. Although I consciously limit my news and social media exposure, I had consumed more than usual in an effort to learn what I could.

I was sitting in my mother's driveway and I received a text from a friend that her 90-year-old mother tested positive for Covid-19. This was the first case of someone that I personally knew, and I was quickly overcome with emotion: crying and praying simultaneously. Maybe you felt that same sense of helplessness in those first few weeks—wondering how to protect the people you love when the whole world seemed uncertain. Maybe you're feeling that sense of helplessness now with whatever you're currently up against.

As I prayed, I was reminded to choose faith over fear. The Holy Spirit helps direct my mind to power, love, and self-control. These are fruits of the Holy Spirit that require me to be *in step* with Him in order to have the fruit of this in my life. I cannot expect to have self-control if I am not connected to the Vine that is producing the fruit.

For this reason I remind you to fan into
flame the gift of God, which is in you through
the laying on of my hands, for God gave us a
spirit not of fear but of power and love and self-control.
2 Timothy 1:6–7

As the weeks passed, we realized this was not a short-term event and we would have to choose how our household would operate. Flint and I both have jobs that are works in progress with building, buying, and selling homes. The responsibilities do not stop just because the government decides to shut everything down. We adapted our work settings, filled our cars with the needed supplies, and set out to continually guide our clients and carry out decisions they made.

My prayer was constantly, "Lord, protect us wherever we go and whatever we do. Grant me a spirit not of fear, but of power and love and self-control." Repeating those words grounded me. This prayer became my anchor when information and emotions swirled. When I am unsure what to pray, either the Lord provides the words in the moment, or He has provided them in the past in His Word so I pray His Word back to Him. Staying connected to the Lord through prayer and Bible reading allows me to continually experience the fruit of the Holy Spirit.

Our church was one of the first in our area to resume worship services in May of 2020 by making modifications to accommodate the seating distance requirements. We also adapted quickly to broadcasting live worship services online and group leaders teaching via YouTube.

Someone at church shared the brilliant idea for us to wear stickers: green if you were open to talking to people and being physically less than 6 feet apart, yellow if you were a bit cautious about that, and red if you wanted to keep the 6 feet no matter what. Isn't that a cool way to share your preferences that allow you to respect another person right where they are? We were all doing our best to acknowledge our own fears and to respect the fears of others. We all have individual experiences that cause fears to develop. And some fears are from something else like losing control or maybe from a physical feeling like an upset stomach with motion sickness. Some fears we are born with and some are developed. Regardless of their origin, the Lord knows each of our fears intimately.

Reminding ourselves of His Word daily (or more often) helps us to hide His words in our heart so that they emerge when we need them most. For years, I desired to have this fruit in my life, but I had to patiently develop it over time by actually reading the Word every day. This is still an area of growth for me as I don't have as many scriptures memorized as I would like. But He is faithful and He helps me recall them so I can pray them as I need them. He also helps plant them into my being just from reading them daily and from listening to songs that include them.

Just this morning, a friend texted me that God is going to get her through her pain. I responded, "Yes, He will," and that brought to my mind the song "Won't He Do It" by We the Kingdom. Within that song, the Word of God is embedded. Perhaps you can memorize Scripture better this way. Whatever ways work, the Lord cares that we are reading or singing His Word to praise Him and proclaim His works to others. This will continually fuel our faith and activate us to overcome our fears.

All of these stories have a thread of faith over fear. Faith requires us to sometimes swim in the opposite direction of many others. We don't want to be reckless, but we also don't want to shrink back from opportunities just because there is an element of risk.

Think about your own life. Does the thought of your young adult child driving home from college at the end of a long week at night make you feel sick? Or you hear an ambulance come down your street and your concern heightens. Maybe going to bed without all your kids at home for the night makes you sleepless. Even everyday fears reveal how deeply we love—and how much we must keep entrusting our loved ones to God.

When I feel sick with concern, I pray. "I know You are with Miriam, Lord. In front of, behind, on each side, above and underneath, hem her in and bring her safely home" (paraphrase of Psalm 139:5). I have fallen asleep praying this. Of course, this was before the days of shared locations. I was thrilled when the noise of Miriam coming down the hall would awaken me. I am so grateful for the Lord answering many of my prayers.

A sturdy home may still creak in a strong wind, but that doesn't mean it's unsafe. The same is true of us—faith doesn't erase fear; it steadies us when fear shakes the walls. When we invite God into every corner of our lives, He restores peace where anxiety once lived.

Reflection Questions

1. What fears have recently "moved in" that I need to ask God to remove?

2. How do I usually respond when fear shows up? Do I fight, freeze, flee, or pray?

3. When have I seen God protect or provide in ways that built my faith?

4. Am I connecting with God regularly by day or by hour as the need warrants?

5. What practices help me replace anxious thoughts with God's promises?

Daily Practice

Choose one verse that strengthens your faith (for example, 2 Timothy 1:7 or Psalm 56:3). Write it on a note, in your phone, and right here in this book. When fear rises, speak that verse aloud as a declaration. End by thanking God for His presence in that exact moment.

Your Turn

Choose one fear you've been carrying lately. Write it down and place it before God. Ask Him to show you one small act of faith you can take today—one step toward trust. Then, as a reminder, write a scripture beside that fear and let it become your declaration of faith.

____

____

____

____

____

____

Prayer

Lord, You know me in every detail. You know every thought (Psalm 139:2) even before I think it. You know every hair on my head; You assigned it a number (Luke 12:7). And You know the exact way that You knit me together in my mother's womb (Psalm 139:13). I know that You also know every fear that I have ever had, those that I have now, and those that I will have in the future. Forgive me for the times I have given in to my fear and let them overcome me. Help me, Lord, to choose to surrender this fear over to You right now. Empower me to choose to rise above this fear and press right into the very territory that makes me afraid. I love You and I trust You. In Jesus' name I pray. Amen.

Threshold to Part 2

In a home, a threshold is the metal, wood, or other material that forms the bottom of a doorway and is necessary to cross over in order to enter the home or the next room. And get this: In the Bible, a threshold symbolizes a transition, an entry that marks a crucial moment in two different states of being. How amazing is that? We are moving from Part 1, "Naming What Hurts You" to Part 2, "Processing the Pain." *These are* crucial moments, and I pray that the Lord empowers you as you read this to allow you to step into the holy place He is preparing for you as you process what He already knows. He will help you learn and make the rough places smooth just as He has done for me.

For much of my 38-year marriage, I have used the words "don't sweep it under the rug" to encourage my husband to have open dialogue with me about whatever is "the problem." A friend shared her feelings about her own marriage. I learned from her that sharing with a trusted friend is important. If we don't talk about the pile of dirt and come up with some way of handling it, tossing it in the trash, or placing it where it needs to go, then it is going to build up. The pile under the rug can only get so high before one of us trips over it. Using those exact words, Flint and I would whittle away at the pile.

Our trauma is similar to that pile under the rug. Hurts can be ignored because we don't *want* to face them or because we don't *know how* to face them. Hurts from childhood might even be ones that are under the rug and we don't even acknowledge them.

The choice is yours. Make deliberate choices to pick up the rug and be courageous enough to take necessary steps. Don't keep tripping. The threshold is here to crossover into learning and tackling the processes that will create an environment for healing to begin. For most, it is a gradual process of healing. Our dependence on Him increases when we surrender more frequently. Day by day, hour by hour, or minute by minute.

A helpful pact to make with yourself is to name what is hurting and try to understand it. Bringing it to the light releases it of its power and thus provides you with freedom. Seek out Christian counselor(s) to help you. Make a list of all the possible resources that can help you. Attend the sessions at intervals that are recommended if possible.

Emotions Wheel

In Parts 2 and 3 we will utilize a tool, the Emotions Wheel. You may have seen it before in other formats. I have seen variations of them in articles online, in books, and in daily planners. This particular Emotions Wheel is found in the *Seeing Jesus Together* Journal[10] created by ICONICITY and is used with their permission. When you are "feeling some kind of way" and cannot identify it or "you have a cloud over your head" and are unsure of its origin, the Emotions Wheel can help. It helps us to process all of our feelings and should be kept in a handy place for daily reference.

---

10 Seeing Jesus Together Journal." *Seeing Jesus Together*, ICONICITY, https://www.seeingjesustogether.com/.

You may also want to purchase your own *Seeing Jesus Together* Journal. More information is in the Resources at the end of this book.

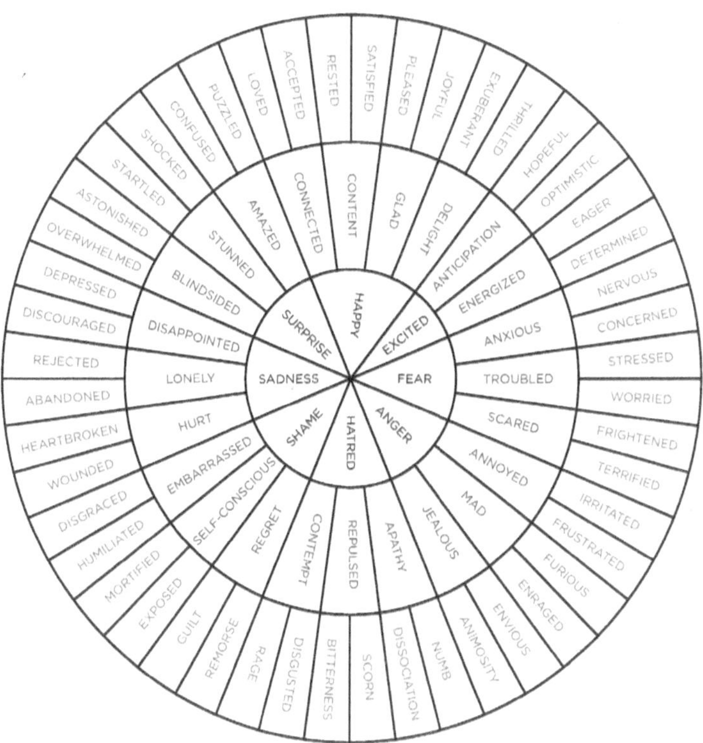

Created in Collaboration with Caleb Grover MA, MDiv, LMHC (www.AgapeACC.com)

PART 2

Moving Through the Mess—Ways to Process the Pain

6

Acknowledging My Feelings

*We cannot selectively numb emotions,
when we numb the painful emotions,
we also numb the positive emotions.*[11]
Brené Brown

When doing a renovation, those in charge may desire (and usually they do) to make the house have certain functions or to have a look it didn't have before. Maybe new plumbing in certain areas or at least new plumbing fixtures, especially in the bathrooms and kitchen. Since changes are being made anyway, they have a vision in mind. Their inspiration uses sketches, maybe old-fashioned magazines, photos, Pinterest boards, and Canva mock-ups for room design and arrangement. It all leads to

---

11 Brown, Brené. *The Gifts of Imperfection: Let Go of Who You Think You're Supposed to Be and Embrace Who You Are.* Hazelden Publishing, 2010.

the home eventually having the look and feel the homeowner desires. The mess of the project is guided by a plan.

Our feelings can be our guide for a few minutes, an hour, or the whole day. Do we want one aspect of our lives to rule over us? That would be like letting the plumber oversee the entire house project. Where would that leave the rest of the house and the vision for its entirety?

If identifying your feelings or any of the words you read becomes overwhelming, think back to the house renovation. Keep in mind the goal for Stewardship of Feelings: to help us move forward through emotions occurring daily. These include everyday emotions plus any that are associated with our trauma experiences.

Be easy on yourself and take a break when needed. Every chapter can stand alone, and reading them in order is not required.

Stewardship of Emotions

Think back to those situations where we might "sweep things under the rug." When we don't truthfully acknowledge the feelings we experience, we sweep feelings *underneath our own rug*. We are not inviting God into our feelings and our stewardship over them. Looking at the Emotions Wheel (see page #) can help us to identify what we are feeling.

When I awake in the morning, my coffee and quiet-time stack (my Bible and journals plus any devotional book I may be reading) are the first things I grab. I write out the statement "Connect with Your Heart" and think about what I am feeling. Some days I am feeling sad because I learned bad news from a friend. Some days I am feeling excited because I am going somewhere I have been planning for a while.

If I cannot identify a feeling, I take a look at the Emotions Wheel for a prompt to my mind that is just being hit by the coffee. I have written that I feel tired more than once as I look back over my journals, but I realize that tiredness is more physical than emotional from my own point of view. Am I tired because I am depressed? Now that *is* an emotion. But that is not the tired I am describing. My tiredness is usually because I did not sleep well, did not go to bed early enough, or awoke earlier than needed and could not return to sleep.

Once identified, I can examine the level of the emotion. Am I being a good steward over the emotions God is giving me? Am I allowing my aggravation with a setting to become full-blown anger? Are my emotions ruling over me and my day, plus all my encounters? If so, then I have allowed my feelings/emotions to dictate my day. When this becomes a habit, my feelings (and thus myself) have a little kingdom set up—an idol competing with my heavenly Father. What an opportunity to confess this to our Lord!

A friend went to a family wedding at a church and as she was meandering through the church in the downtime prior to the wedding, she stumbled on a budget basket of journals and picked one up for $5.00. She brought that journal to share with me and our church and I love it! *Seeing Jesus Together* is the name of the journal. What I learned in the process of using their journaling strategy is that we need to be good stewards over our emotions. In order to be a good steward, we have to assess what is present. The journal provides the prompt: "Connect with your heart. Write a few 'I feel' statements."

The practice of writing these "I feel" statements allows them to be ordered in our minds, submitted to God's control. And confessed to Him when realizing that an emotion is out of line with His commands.

On a given day, I have realized that I am giving too much of myself through feelings and emotions to a situation that irritates me. Turn to the Emotions Wheel to look up the emotion "Irritation." The extended emotion of "irritation" is "annoyed," and then according to the wheel, it becomes full-blown "anger."

From this self-examination, I notice that the situation is irritating me now. As I consider that, God allows His words to come into my mind: "Set your minds on things that are above, not on things that are on earth" (Colossians 3:2). From His power I am able to realize my mistake of being irritated by something that is insignificant. I whisper breath prayers to God asking for forgiveness for letting my emotions get out of hand and asking Him to help me keep my emotions under His control. That self-control is a fruit of the power of the Holy Spirit in me. I am choosing to surrender running away with my irritated feelings and instead releasing them to His control.

Full of Feelings

By age 59, I had never had surgery. Because I served on staff at our church, I have prayed with countless people who were about to have surgery. Luckily, I had avoided it.

Several years ago, I was putting trash into a can, turned around, and stumped my left foot on a concrete ledge I had not noticed. The pain was excruciating at the moment. Within a few days, the bruising was evident on my big toe and foot. I knew from experience that there isn't a lot that helps a broken toe. I simply carried on until the pain began to affect my ability to walk.

At my first surgical consult, I decided not to use that surgeon. I sought a foot expert instead. When I met him, he explained everything and told me to call to schedule the surgery date. I decided to delay until the pain was unbearable.

Two years passed. I turned down opportunities to go on walks with friends, adjusted my weightlifting, and continued to make modifications that allowed me to endure. One day, I realized I couldn't get down on the floor to play with my granddaughter if my foot was impaired. I scheduled another appointment with the foot specialist and booked the surgery.

Although I was nervous about it, I knew this was the best path. It would provide the greatest chance of walking and being active over the next twenty years. However, it was much more difficult than I anticipated. The inability to bear weight was minimized (maybe by me in my own mind). My husband and I thought it would be simple. I didn't think twice about saying, "Sure, play in that golf tournament the weekend following surgery." Boy, were we wrong. I didn't ask enough questions or interview enough people who had similar surgeries. We sought the help of friends who are medical professionals and called on friends and family to gather all the things that we *should have known* to have prior to surgery. Crutches, a walker, a scooter, bathing wipes, bandages, ankle wrap, over the counter meds. You name it, I needed it. Oh, and we also signed the dog up for a week at the kennel because I couldn't get up every five minutes to let him in or out!

On postoperative day 5, a particular accident caused me to be *full* of feelings. It was a great morning and my daughter had taken me to get my hair washed and cut. It's the kind of thing that makes anyone feel better. A big high with a great morning, and then a big low happened.

I took a terrible fall from a knee scooter. Really, it happened so fast, I just knew I was falling toward an armoire and smashed into it with the left side of my head. Specifically, my ear took the full weight of my body's impact. My left knee hit the floor hard under my weight and the weight of the scooter. The inside of my right leg had fallen on top of the scooter. These were all pain points.

Slowly I moved. And said aloud, "I don't want this to be me. I don't want this to be me." I could feel the throbbing pain from my head and ear. Twice I nearly raised myself up on my recovering foot and consciously stopped to make my body obey and use the other "good" foot.

My right foot needed to be the weight-bearing foot so I could stand. I used the bed as a steadying force. "I don't want this to be me." Half crying, I composed myself and shuffled to the bathroom while trying to keep with the recovery instructions of "heel weight only for the left foot." My thoughts were blurry. I needed to assess my situation, so I made a video of my injured ear and narrated it to my daughter in hopes that she could tell me the condition.

Then I remembered I could watch the video myself! I took care of the injury the best I could while limping around on my one good foot. My head was hurting, too, so I laid down on the bed to give myself time to relax and attempt to think clearly.

I was having a hard time accepting that I just had a "wreck" on the scooter that is supposed to be helping me. My, how things change in the blink of an eye. My ego was bruised along with my ear, head, and both of my knees. I pulled myself up, then texted my daughter and my husband.

"Glad you are ok. Do you want me to come over?"

"No, I'm ok," I texted back. But I am also asking myself, *Am I really okay?*

I am a very active person with zero health issues. The same person who chose to have this proactive surgery in hopes of maintaining my mobility into my 80s and 90s. But at that moment I was not active. I used a lot of my energy simply to go to the bathroom. I needed a lineup of items around the recliner so they are within arm's reach for the times I am alone… which is most of the day! My expectations of myself were not matching my reality. Have you ever been in the same situation? A transition period for our minds is necessary when our expectations don't match reality.

Normally, I relish time alone. Suddenly it was overwhelming to have a whole day looming before me with no plans to be with people. *I don't want this to be me.* My mind was having a hard time accepting my current state.

The next morning, I wrote in my journal: "I feel surprised because of the challenge of this recovery." (This is postoperative day 6 and I am now admitting this to myself.) "I feel overwhelmed because of the many facets of it." Never have I felt like I needed to write "brush my teeth" on a to-do list, but literally, I had forgotten twice until nearly lunch time and couldn't believe I did that. "I feel blindsided because the expectations I had were wrong. I feel regret because I did not ask more questions. I feel the need to find determination and resolve because I need to get through this."

If I don't take the time to admit my feelings, it is more difficult to move forward. I find myself grumpy and generally in a worse mood. If I shove them under the rug, I am likely to trip over them when I least expect it. (Like a blowup over not being able to *find* my toothbrush, my car keys, or perhaps burning dinner… how insignificant is that?) But it won't be insignificant if there is a blowup. It will affect myself and others present. It will affect my activities and interactions for this day. It will damage my Christian witness and my purpose to make Him known to others. It goes against God's Word. It is sinful.

I cannot afford to miss even one day and allow myself to get out of line when I can avoid it through this small daily practice. My witness matters too much and so does yours.

There will still be times when our emotions spiral and surprise us, but we can examine ourselves and confess it to the Lord. Submitting our emotions to Him will allow the surprises to be less frequent.

The next step in the journal is to *surrender to the Lord through prayer*. Again, from my journal I wrote: Lord, I surrender my mind today. I surrender my time and all of my focus. I am such a wimp! I surrender my bad attitude. I surrender all my ridiculous thoughts. I want to be stronger than this. Lord, help me to surrender this bad attitude. There is nothing I can experience where You won't be with me. You will never leave me or forsake me.

As I ponder this written surrender, I realize that I need to be in my community of believers. Perhaps the Lord brought this to my mind. I hadn't been to church in two Sundays because of the surgery. And I never miss, because worshipping with my church family is such a boost to me every single week. It encourages my faith and helps me be more bold for His kingdom's work. *Going to my small group will help.*

In order to help bring my feelings under control, I followed my journal entry with a text to a friend to ask for a ride to our small group meeting. I wasn't planning to go because it just seemed like too many steps to take to get myself ready and get there. I literally made myself get up, go take my "hospital-wipe bath," get dressed, and gather my study materials. Now to get myself out the door and sit outside to wait for my ride. I felt like a kid waiting on the school bus. All dressed, but a little apprehensive about how this would all go.

These are all feelings that were moving quickly. God is sovereign over our emotions, and if I am allowing them to be out of control, I am unable to fulfill His purposes for this moment in time—and easily my entire day—if I let them run away from me. A fruit of His Spirit in us is self-control, and I want to equip myself with this daily.

I am grateful for the process to help me know that my feelings do not dominate me. He provides strength in this process to help us become better stewards over our feelings.

The time with my small group was great! It was so good to be cared for by my friends—each one meeting a need whether I expressed it or not. One shared a testimony, one drove me to our group, a different one drove me home and cleaned up my ear plus helped me get my lunch and get settled back in my chair. The body of Christ was at work doing what the body is supposed to do, and I am so grateful to tears even now knowing that "Yes, this is me. I *do want* this to be me. I want to be the overcomer that God has made me to be."

He gave me strength as I identified my feelings. He gave me determination to steward my feelings and not allow them to escalate and dominate me or my day. In my surrender He helped me to see that I don't have to wallow in this new place. I can make it a place of rest and thus restoration.

Clearly times of change are challenging, but humbling myself before the Lord, being transparent with my feelings, confessing them to Him, and surrendering the "I don't want this to be me" attitude allowed the space for His Holy Spirit to turn me around from defeat to determination. My heart was feeling one way and my head (plus God's Spirit in me) knew I needed an adjustment. We cannot simply accept and wallow in our emotions just because we feel a feeling in our heart. The Bible explains that in this verse:

> The heart is deceitful above all things,
> and desperately sick; who can understand it?
> Jeremiah 17:9

We cannot be expected to understand it, but we can acknowledge that it is deceitful and sick. So if it is sick, I want to reconsider everything "it" tells me through my emotions.

Consider the household renovation. The vision of the project is followed by the plans to implement the vision. Day by day, small pieces of the project take place in order to bring the entire project to completion. Our lives are similar to that. You can follow these plans that help you become a steward of your feelings. Day by day, you may not notice a big change; but then after a few weeks, the fruit of your consistent efforts will become noticeable through more personal peace and greater satisfaction in your self-awareness and your relationships.

Reflection Questions

1. Am I being honest and transparent with myself?

2. Am I willing to admit how I really feel? Or am I covering it up?

3. Am I glossing over my feelings so I don't really have to examine where this is coming from?

Daily Practice

I am no psychologist, but I do know that this daily practice of "Connecting with Our Heart" over the past year has helped me realize that I need the Lord's help in responding to circumstances. Not just the appropriate emotion, but the *level* of that emotion. "Leveling down" is what some would call it. Stewarding my emotions helps me to become more Christ-like.

The repetition of this daily examination of my feelings grants me rest and peace from the busyness in my mind as I reflect on my emotions. Not only do I feel peace, but also freedom. This freedom allows me to explore self-control as I surrender these feelings to the Lord day by day.

Your Turn

Take a look at the Emotions Wheel's outer edge. (See Emotions Wheel on page 55) Look for emotions that accurately describe the way you feel at this moment or have felt in the last day. As the feelings are named and are listed toward the inner part of the circle, write down that emotion. It helps to follow that emotion to the center and see what this emotion can become when escalated without careful stewardship. This can help us to realize the origin of that emotion. It is possible to explore that in prayer with the Lord. Resist choosing emotions on the wheel that are *how you would like to feel* and pick ones that honestly describe you at this moment.

Prayerfully articulate what you are feeling and why.
Examples:

I feel / felt sad because I forgot my friend's birthday.
I feel / felt disappointed because we lost the football game.

I feel / felt ______________ (emotion) because ______________
(circumstance).

____

____

I feel / felt ______________ (emotion) because ______________
(circumstance).

____

____

I feel / felt ______________ (emotion) because ______________
(circumstance).

____

____

If this pace or rhythm of writing is doable for you, considering
beginning your day journaling two or three I feel statements.

Prayer

Lord Jesus, thank You for Your sovereignty over everything and for creating me uniquely even with the giving of our emotions. I read in Your Word about Your emotions of joy (John 15:11), sorrow and grief (Isaiah 53:3), and even anger (Mark 3:5). I know, Lord, that You intend for me to be the steward of my emotions rather than allowing my emotions to rule over me. Forgive me when I allow or have allowed my emotions to rule me, my day, or my circumstances. "Make me know your ways, O LORD; teach me your paths. Lead me in your truth and teach me, for you are the God of my salvation; for you I wait all day long" (Psalm 25:4–5). In Jesus' name I pray. Amen.

7

The Sacred Pause

Doing those deeply unfashionable things—
slowing down, letting your spare time expand, getting enough sleep,
resting—is a radical act now, but it is essential.[12]

A well built home or a renovation done right is one of seasoned craftsmanship that takes time. A lot of people will tell me they don't want a cookie-cutter house. These are built in neighborhoods where they build a whole street filled with homes at the same time, with plans that are very similar, and maybe a few exterior changes are the only differences between the homes.

Homes like this are built quickly, and after five years, there are often visible signs of the lack of skilled craftsmanship and high-quality materials. Homes that are built individually by people who have done the trade for decades are built to last. When it is time for a remodel, the floors are still level because the original foundation was done with the best available materials and practices passed down across generations.

---

12 May, Katherine. *Wintering: The Power of Rest and Retreat in Difficult Times.* Riverhead Books, 2020.

The point of the anchor home here is to SLOW DOWN so there is room for optimal healing. Ironically, healing often happens more fully and steadily when we allow life to move at a snail's pace. You get to define the speed of the snail, which may change from day to day depending on your energy. Just like a well-built home requires patient craftsmanship, seasons of grief and caregiving invite us to embrace a slower, more intentional rhythm.

Old-Fashioned Ways

Following my Dad's passing in 2020, my mom was at my house for a few weeks at a time. On higher energy days, going slow wasn't stepping away for rest. It was standing shoulder to shoulder in my kitchen, mixing pound cake batter. A friend had delivered a pound cake to our family, and weeks later we were still talking about it. I knew it would be good therapy for Mom and I for her to help me perfect my cake baking.

She loved some of the old ways of doing things that she had always done—like measuring all the ingredients out in advance. She wanted each individual ingredient in shallow bowls carefully covered with a paper towel. Butter and eggs sat out, too, so they would be at room temperature just right for mixing up. Some old-fashioned ways she was willing to give up like stirring by hand. Using my stand mixer was an easy transition for her to avoid her shoulder pain from stirring. We planned everything out the night before and covered the countertops with all the bowls in the correct order for mixing, just like she prefers. No baking late in the day, no microwaves, no rushing. "You have to cream the butter, sugar, and Crisco *until it's light and fluffy,*" she'd say, holding the wooden spoon like a baton of wisdom.

In those quiet moments, a flour-dusted kitchen was cleaned as we worked, because "everything has its place." I learned something deeper: Slowing down isn't always a sabbatical. It is not always a preplanned retreat. It's choosing to go slowly for a few hours when the world would rather you hurry and grab a cake from the local grocery store. Caregiving and grieving became less about a task to endure and more about *being present* with one another. I was able to listen to Mom's stories and honor her preferences. I realized that love and rest often sound like the oven door closing on a cake ready to bake, a kitchen cleaned, and going to "sit for a spell."

With Mom's gentle direction, we perfected my cake-baking that spring, baking at least one cake a week until I had it just right. These were none other than Sundrop Pound Cakes, and you can find the recipe inside the front cover. Slow mornings didn't just produce perfect cakes. They were quietly rebuilding something in me too. Jesus' words came alive in a new way for me. Like sitting with my mama and Jesus at the same time. A time when we both felt the burden of loss—loss of my dad, loss in the pandemic, and loss of time with other people. Those heavy cares were surrendered through the ordinary days of baking cakes and brought needed rest. We were baking because we wanted to, not because we had to. Are you resting because you want to? Or because you have to? In the book of Matthew, Jesus extends us an invitation to rest.

> Come to me, all who labor and are heavy laden,
> and I will give you rest.
> Take my yoke upon you, and learn from me,
> for I am gentle and lowly in heart,
> and you will find rest for your souls.
> For my yoke is easy, and my burden is light.
> Matthew 11:28–30

Slowing down also gave us space to explore questions we'd never taken time to ask before. Honestly, I had not even thought of these things until Storyworth (see the Resources) gave me the idea. I asked Mom their prompts about her childhood and days spent with Dad and other family members. My sister, Jackie, would probe a bit more with more specific questions if Mom wasn't understanding. And I typed away in order to record her answers in her words. I was careful to use Mom's phrasing. It captures more of the essence of who she is. This was great therapy for all of us.

I think Mom enjoyed reliving her memories, as she became animated and very descriptive while answering the questions. She told us things we had never heard before and we enjoyed her sprinkling of humor. In one of the stories about "My Favorite Drink," she surprised us with an IW Harper. Then she teased that it was an alcoholic beverage and we laughed because Mom never drank any alcohol except wine at the Communion Table.

We spent many afternoons quizzing her using the ideas Storyworth gave us. Sometimes if their prompts didn't apply to Mom's life, we would make up our own. This resulted in a collection of eighteen of her stories. Some of the details may have blurred with time, but they're *her* stories. Precious memories for us to cherish. The "what makes me happy" memories went from peanut butter crackers and a Pepsi-Cola to driving the tractor in Concord with her father. She smiled a lot when describing "chasing your daddy" and then got serious with "what makes me happy is knowing Jesus and knowing where I am going when I leave this world."

I pieced together Mom's words in those stories on Storyworth. It gave me an opportunity to reflect on the stories of my own life. Industrialization of America has been good in some regards because we are able to *choose to* pursue our own healing journey. And I have this opportunity to slowly write this book in order to help you and me. I don't think my mom ever had those luxuries.

Just like a seasoned builder doesn't rush the foundation, our hearts need time to settle, become steady, and strengthen. In this season, I discovered a slower rhythm that became sacred space—where legacy was shared, faith deepened, and healing quietly unfolded.

Reflection Questions

1. Do you choose to slow down? If not, why not?

2. What creativity would you like to explore?

3. Does slowing down bring about thoughts of the very thing that needs to be faced? What are your thoughts that arise?

4. What in your life that does not have an eternal impact can be eliminated?

Daily Practice

Choose one of your daily activities—preparing a meal, folding laundry, or taking a walk—and do it slowly, without multitasking. Go for a long walk and leave your phone at home. Notice what surfaces in the quiet: thoughts to explore in journaling, a family recipe to be made and enjoyed, conversations to have, prayers to be written or spoken aloud?

Your Turn

With whatever arises to the surface, will you pray for the courage to act on it? Some of the steps that come to your mind may be the very gift to open the next door in your journey. Listening to the song lyrics of "Not in a Hurry" by Will Reagan / United Pursuit are so helpful to me when I have allowed myself to be too influenced by the world. Don't rush ahead in my own strength when I can rely on the Holy Spirit instead. Do you feel like that too? Listen to the full version linked in the Resources. You, too, will begin to notice where God is speaking to you through the circumstances of your own life.

Prayer

Lord, I praise You for being our God, never in a hurry. You desire for me to be clothed in strength and dignity, to receive and share wisdom (Proverbs 31:25–26), and as my Creator, You know what I need better than I do. Forgive me when I have thought that I know best. Forgive me for running ahead of You and trying to keep pace with a busy world. Thank You for allowing me to experience the presence of Your Holy Spirit in still, small moments that help me know You more deeply. Show me the next steps and give me the courage to face and be set free by the truth in Your Word. In Jesus' name I pray. Amen.

8

Freedom From Blame

You cannot solve a problem until you acknowledge that you have one and accept responsibility for solving it.[13]
Zig Ziglar

Upon examination of a home, one can quickly notice that each system of the home, like electrical, plumbing, and HVAC, has a particular purpose that works best in a particular place. Many consider the hot water heater location in the crawl space in case of a leak or the HVAC elevated from the ground for geographical areas that flood easily. The garage is on the end of the house that is most level with the ground. There is a purpose for everything and a particular location that works best for that purpose. The builder controls the locations where it is possible and incorporates the homeowner's requests.

---

13 Ziglar, Zig. *Over the Top: Moving from Survival to Stability, from Stability to Success, from Success to Significance.* Thomas Nelson Inc., 1997, p. 191.

Sometimes, a tension exists because the builder knows the best practices, but that may not be the outcome desired by the homeowner. It is an opportunity for education. Builders are not always teachers, so it can get a little sticky. If the builder is not a skilled communicator, "someone can get the blame." You, the homeowner, have the final authority. Just like you the person makes the final decision in whether or not you will heed the recommendations given.

Failure of the AED

Let's revisit the day of my son's high school wrestling match at Forest Hills High School. The trauma experienced on this particular day is not meant to be compared to traumas that have been endured over time or traumas that were personally abusive. Since that is not my experience, I can direct you to helpful counselors in the Resources at the end of this book. I do acknowledge the pain and the experiences that the innocent have endured. I have personally served survivors of such atrocities. This is not the same.

In our area, an athletic trainer is responsible for the medical equipment and first aid for the teams present at his school, whether at an open field or the gymnasium. Athletic trainers are employed in partnership between the school system and the hospital system. Once the coaches realized an AED (automatic external defibrillator) was needed for our son, the athletic director went to retrieve it although it should have been present. It was not in ready-to-use condition and the adult leads were missing.

Therefore, those making decisions chose not to use the pediatric leads. Our son wrestled in the 185 pound weight class and was 5'10" at the time, so it is certainly understandable to consider only adult leads for potential success.

What about the non-working AED? In the weeks that followed, emails and messages both verbal and via text came to me about our retribution in the situation. By pointing out things I had not known and was in no position to handle, it was an unnecessary distraction, so I just put it out of my mind. Our focus was on celebrating this miracle and doing all we could to help our son. Honestly, we felt the Holy Spirit hover over us constantly for weeks following the incident.

The school's athletic trainer, who was known for his longevity, accolades, and dedication to his career, was dismissed from his position. We were not told the reason, but many presumed it was because of the faulty AED equipment. Well-meaning friends and acquaintances recommended we file a lawsuit against the hospital who employed him. This would be the very hospital who also served us well during our emergency arrival, surgery, and recovery just 14 days earlier. I couldn't even consider such an idea.

I could not fathom retribution against this athletic trainer. My entire being knew if he were dedicated to his career, the "punishment" of losing his job was more than enough. There was no question for us that we would not be pursuing a lawsuit of any kind.

Human nature makes us want to blame someone. We want to see someone suffer for the wrong that has occurred. Or perhaps in another setting, one would blame themselves. What were the signs that I had missed? The previous year, we had completed a battery of tests to make sure the heart tests were acceptable and they were, but tests can be wrong.

Whether it is an inaccurate test or the oversight of a human, it is never easy to overlook an offense committed against us or someone we love. As our compassion grows with our commitment to the Lord, our hearts break for even innocent strangers who are suffering because of the unjust actions of another. Knowing the Lord, His Word, and His ways continually shapes us into His likeness. Because my heart belongs to the Lord and His Word dwells within me, His words flood my mind: What does the Lord say?

> Vengeance is mine, I will repay, says the Lord.
> Romans 12:19b
> Good sense makes one slow to anger,
> and it is his glory to overlook an offense.
> Proverbs 19:11
> As for you, you meant evil against me,
> but God meant it for good.
> Genesis 50:20a
> My son, be attentive to my words;
> incline your ear to my sayings.
> Let them not escape from your sight;
> keep them within your heart.
> For they are life to those who find them,
> and healing to all their flesh.
> Proverbs 4:20–22

Return in your mind to the house metaphor. Reacquaint your mind with the builder who knows the best outcome for the restoration project and imagine yourself as the homeowner who has a different outcome in mind. Now tell your mind to think of the builder as the Lord and you are the owner of your life. Just like the homeowner, we sometimes have our own agenda or a desired outcome predetermined. As followers of Jesus, we must allow His way to reign in our life and our body (our "house"). The outcomes that we create in our minds must be surrendered to Him. Our plans not coming together often means He has a better plan. Release control and focus on His

Word to us as *supreme* over our own thoughts. Because we have the Holy Spirit to help us, we can relinquish our thoughts and our mentally created outcomes to His authority.

Reflection Questions

1. What keeps us from inviting the Lord into all of our decisions?

2. Where or what gives us the idea that our way is the best way?

3. How can we recognize God's plans?

> For my thoughts are not your thoughts, neither are
> your ways my ways, declares the LORD.
> For as the heavens are higher than the earth,
> so are my ways higher than your ways
> and my thoughts than your thoughts.
> Isaiah 55:8–9

In order to move from being one who desires revenge to one who can release it to the Lord, only the power of the Holy Spirit and the Word of God can transform. He shapes our character into His likeness in an instant or over time. We don't get to choose and we never know how this transformation will occur. We are simply called to be obedient to Him.

If you love me, you will
keep my commandments.
John 14:15

Daily Practice

If daily reading of the Word and prayer is not already a habit, prayerfully consider adding this as soon as you are able. You can begin with reading a shorter devotional to accommodate the shortened attention span of a person healing from trauma (See Resource Page). Read His Word daily and ask for His help according to His Word through prayer.

Your Turn

Practice "I feel" statements related to blame if this applies in your situation. Review the Emotions Wheel on page 55 to identify the emotions for your I feel statements.

Additionally, the I feel statements are your new method for processing feelings that arise and you may not know what to do with them. Instead of worrying, pondering, and wondering how to handle them on your own, release them to the Lord through your writing.

Example: I feel sad because this former friend cannot have a relationship without attempting to control everything.

I feel / felt _____________ (emotion) because _______________ (circumstance).

____

____

I feel / felt ______________ (emotion) because ________________ (circumstance).

____

____

I feel / felt ______________ (emotion) because ________________ (circumstance).

____

____

Prayer

Thank you, Lord, for Your Word and the way You allow me, by the power of Your Holy Spirit, to be changed by it daily. Grant me the discipline and fortitude to continually read the Bible and pray to You everyday. Forgive me for the times I have failed to seek You first. Forgive me for blaming others when I don't know the truth. And when I do know the truth, Lord, help me forgive them too. Lord, help me to let go of any of the blame I may feel in the experiences that I have endured. Help me to release all of it to You and to be a good steward over the feelings that are associated with revenge. Allow me to overlook the mistakes of others. I want to fully embrace the freedom that comes from forgiving another person. Thank You for the freedom of forgiveness. Thank You for Your Word and the truth it brings to my heart. Change my heart where change is needed and shape me more into Your likeness today. In Jesus' name I pray. Amen.

9

The Gift of Honest Companionship

---

*We were created for community, fashioned for fellowship,
and formed for a family, and none of us can fulfill God's
purposes by ourselves.[14]*
Rick Warren

Our world often celebrates independence, thus true spiritual companionship is a rare and beautiful gift—like the carefully crafted framework of a strong home. In a well-built home, the framing is what gives shape and strength to everything else. Stud walls, beams, and braces create a skeleton that allows the house to stand tall and true.

Framing isn't done alone—each piece must be measured, aligned, and connected to others so the entire structure can bear the load together. If one wall stands apart, the house

---

14 Warren, Rick. *The Purpose Driven Life: What on Earth Am I Here For?* Zondervan, 2002.

cannot hold. In the same way, a faithful life built in isolation can't bear the full weight of life's storms.

Community that provides a safe place for sharing can become a wonderful tool for accountability. Our faith and healing grow stronger when joined with others who help us hold steady. For me, the aspect of accountability fulfills such a great need. I desired and prayed for a group for a long time before I actually had one. I could see the benefits of it for the students in our youth group and I *so wanted* that same thing, but at the time, we did not have the systems in place within our church to help adult groups meet and grow.

Formation of a Small Group

Our small group began meeting at the home of a friend. We started in the book of James, as our whole church was studying it at the time. There were just a few of us, maybe three or four. We met at the same time every week so that we could all adjust our schedules and plan around our time together in order to all be present as regularly as possible.

We would bring a few Bible study books to the group and all the ladies would look them over and we would decide our next study. When the study would wrap up in the month of May, we would take a break for the summer since we would all be away at various times. We quickly learned that we didn't want to continue that practice because the absence from one another broke up our rhythm. It would take months to regain the momentum of regularly meeting to encourage one another when we restarted in the fall months.

> And let us consider how to stir up one another
> to love and good works,

not neglecting to meet together, as is the habit of some,
but encouraging one another,
and all the more as you see the Day drawing near.
Hebrews 10:24–25

Around the holidays, we would take turns meeting in the homes of one another for a greater opportunity to know one another more deeply. One of my favorite memories is the year we went house to house to help one another decorate our Christmas trees. What a joy to do that together.

In 2013, just days after Matthew's discharge from the hospital, our group invited us over for dinner. We had not gone anywhere yet because we didn't feel we had the capacity for that. Yet, the safety and security of our group (and their husbands) was the perfect landing for a brief reintroduction to normal life.

At some point, we developed a text thread managed by one of the gals in our group. We use it for prayer requests while we are away from one another. It is incredible how many prayers come from within this group in a week's time, and it is equally amazing how God shows up within those requests. Any time there has been a particularly challenging need presented during our group time, we gather around that person to lay hands on them in prayer. I just love the grace-filled moments we have shared with one another. Even when we're not physically together, that thread acts like hidden beams running through the walls of the house—quietly holding things in place.

As the Holy Spirit bound us together, the ambition to lead developed within a variety of our group members. We moved to a "rotating facilitator" type model for our group organically. One day while we were studying the book of Acts, I asked who among the group might like to facilitate the next lesson and five different people volunteered. How amazing is God to raise up leaders within our group for the purposes of facilitating lessons that help us all grow? We get the additional perspective of a different leader, a different point of view, variety in study style, and facilitating talents. It has been a beautiful gift that came as we studied the very scriptures in Acts that tell us about the multiplication of the church!

We all agreed simultaneously that we love the improvements to our group dynamics by studying a book of the Bible rather than choosing a "Bible study." The scripture is easier for all of us to assimilate into our lives, and the Bible studies were very time consuming with no greater gain. We would find ourselves individually spending hours looking up various parts of scriptures, reading, watching the author's hour-long video, and answering pages of discussion questions. After taking a break from that workbook methodology, all of us in the group (an average of 12 people weekly) decided we gain just as much biblical wisdom in less time using a book of the Bible and a short conversational commentary. This could result as a fruit from our past Bible study experiences that have allowed us to reach this point. Or it could be for God's purposes in the leadership development of our group for this season of our lives. Hopefully, these insights help your group in deciding collectively how to pursue growth.

There are responsibilities of each group member. We keep confidentiality of prayer requests and group discussions. We read the Word and pray for one another. Obviously we want everyone to show up each week, but perfection is not the goal. Relationships are the goal: growing relationships with the Lord and with one another. Our transformation as a group is evident in the fruit of the individuals in the group. We don't really pursue group projects, but each of us serves the kingdom according to the needs in front of us at the time and the talent that the Lord has given each of us.

I asked the ladies the value of our group in their life. Here are their answers:

- It keeps me accountable to reading God's Word and preparing for our Bible study.
- Praying for the needs of people I don't know makes my world seem smaller, yet larger!
- It keeps me grounded.
- It encourages more deliberate and intentional study of God's Word, which results in a deeper relationship and understanding of God. It enables me to have different perspectives of God's truth, and it fosters friendships and unity with people I would not have known before.
- It helps me see the beauty and potential of God's church.
- I love interacting with others as they share their hearts, thoughts, and needs. The "protective walls" come down and you can love them for who they are.
- I know I can confide in you ladies.
- Seeing God work in others' lives helps me love others better.
- If I am struggling, the group helps me keep my head above water.
- I know you will be there for my problems as I am there for yours.
- The group gives me conviction and discipline that I wasn't even aware I needed. Like when I need to slow down and be present to listen or when I need to speed up and get to work.
- I realize I am not the only one going through something because someone in the group has experienced the same thing.
- It is a safe place where I am not judged.

- The group helps me see things in a different light, removing the blinders so I can see more clearly how God is working in my situation.
- I never felt "new" even when I was new to the group. I felt accepted from Day 1.
- I look forward to our weekly meetings & discussions.
- I know I have prayer warriors instantly and can feel the love and prayers.
- As seasons of lives change, so do the faces in our group. Some people have a job change, location change, or are called to another group. However, our group remains consistent, faithful, and flourishing. And always welcoming to new people who want to be in a group.

Just as a home's frame depends on each beam being joined to the others, our spiritual lives are strengthened when we're connected to honest companions. Week after week, this small group has become part of the structure holding me steady—a framework of prayer, accountability, and shared faith that allows each of us to stand stronger than we could alone.

Reflection Questions

1. Who has been part of the "framework" that supports your spiritual growth?

2. In what ways have you experienced accountability as a *gift* rather than a burden?

3. Are there areas where God might be inviting you to step into deeper companionship or community?

4. How might you offer honest support to someone else this week?

Daily Practice

Reach out to one person from your faith community this week—thank them for the way they've supported you, or ask how you can be praying for them. If you don't have a small group, take one step toward finding or forming one. We have quite a few ladies in our group who do not attend our church. Through personal relationships and social media posts about our upcoming study, conversations start about our small group. People are curious. Although many of the ladies attend a variety of churches, we welcome everyone who desires to know Jesus and His Word. You likely have some friends who are in a group already. One lady came to us from our website, so push yourself a little out of your comfort zone. Check out the website of churches near you. The results will be worth it and *we are* one body in Christ.

Your Turn

If you have a trusted group already, praise the Lord! Continue pursuing Bible study and prayer with the group and pray for one another when you are not together. Encourage transparency by being more transparent with your own sharing and prayer requests. It is amazing to see God at work in the midst of the group.

If you do not have a group, do not be afraid to start small. That is the best way. Ask the Lord to help you find one faithful person who will meet regularly. Trust the Lord to build it from there. Be patient. The group I am now in started approximately twelve years ago, and I had the desire and prayer for it for at least five years before that.

Prayer

Lord, thank You for the gift of honest companionship. Thank You for the people who have framed and strengthened my faith through their prayers, encouragement, and presence. Forgive me when I have not been the same for someone else. Lord, for those without a group, bring them together with others who are craving the same godly companionship. Grant them patience to wait for You and to be faithful in seeking You in the opportunities they do have. Help me to walk in humility and openness, to give and receive support, and to keep showing up for the people You've placed in my life. Knit our hearts together in Your love, and build something lasting among us. In Jesus' name, Amen.

10

From Retaliation to Release

A man that studieth revenge keepeth his own wounds green,
which otherwise would heal and do well.[15]
Francis Bacon

When building a custom house, circumstances often don't go according to plan. There will be challenges that we don't expect to face. When we are not getting what we want or what we sense is justified, how do we handle it? If the windows come in and the size isn't correct, we don't yell at the general contractor or expect to smash the windows in an attempt to make them fit. Yelling at the general contractor might feel satisfying at the moment, but it doesn't solve the problem. In fact, it creates more damage to repair. Retaliation promises relief, but release is where true healing begins.

---

15 Bacon, Francis. "Of Revenge." *Essays or Counsels, Civil and Moral,* 1625.

Somebody Will Pay for This!

Around 1990, I worked for a cosmetic company and traveled with them to regional events for the independent contractors in that area. We held them in late winter and this particularly cold and snowy February in Massachusetts found me ready to head south after the training institute was finished. We worked long hours in dress clothing with heels and my feet were killing me. There was not enough sleep due to the long hours, plentiful work to be done, and conversations with lots of people.

We were awaiting airport transportation so we could all get to our favorite destinations, our homes. Several of my co-workers and I rolled our luggage out to the curb for pickup. A University of Massachusetts van pulled into the pull-thru parking area and literally ran over my suitcase. We all stood there in disbelief as the van kept rolling like it didn't just smash a 50-pound bag. I was livid. My friends who witnessed it can still imitate me furiously stating, "Somebody's gonna pay for this!" It always comes up with laughter when we are together.

Logically, demanding someone "pay for this" would help in the future, but it did nothing in the moment. My bag was smashed, its contents broken—especially fragile cosmetics that spilled and ruined the rest. Good news: The university paid for the bag and the damaged contents. Bad news: It took several months to get it worked out. Wouldn't it be nice if the injustices of the world were wrapped with a bow in a few short months? Injustice often feels like that crushed suitcase—something valuable has been damaged, and our first instinct is to demand immediate payback.

My broken suitcase was eventually paid for and my reeling emotions calmed, but what about when the wrong is bigger, deeper, or written into law itself? What about injustices no insurance claim can fix? God does not partner with wicked rulers. He is not swayed by political power, human systems, or legal loopholes. His justice stands firm, even when earthly systems falter.

> Can wicked rulers be allied with you,
> those who frame injustice by statute?
> Psalm 94:20

When injustice becomes institutionalized—whether through unfair laws, corrupt leadership, or systems that harm the vulnerable—it can feel overwhelming and even hopeless. But this verse anchors us in God's character: He cannot and will not align Himself with evil. His throne is established on righteousness and justice.

> Righteousness and justice are the foundation of your throne;
> steadfast love and faithfulness go before you.
> Psalm 89:14

Rebuilding one's life is the goal, and retaliation is like trying to rebuild using the wrong materials. When we are not building on the foundation of God's character, our outcome will be the house built on sinking sand. It may have merit in the moment that makes your flesh feel better because you see someone else suffering instead of or in addition to you. But that won't last. The sinking sand of the faulty foundation will give way to the structure, and the suffering of all will still remain.

In all of life, this *will happen*. There *will be a storm* or many over our decades. You will endure it personally or you will accompany someone in their suffering . The way you respond to the storm will depend on your worldview. Think of it like carrying a cup of coffee over to your chair. If you do this every day, there will at some point be a *bump*. The bump will be something that causes the coffee to spill. Maybe you trip on the rug. Maybe the dog gets under your feet. Maybe the cup is a bit too full. Maybe you're in a hurry. Regardless of what causes the *bump*, your response to it will affect you and those around. You will either blunder the situation or clean it up, make another cup, and carry on. You will have an appropriate response to the *bump*. Handling the *bumps* of life with a biblical worldview becomes part of the framework of your life from having practiced it.

The way to practice this sort of thing is to read the Word daily and apply it to your life. Being in step with the Holy Spirit and responding to *the bumps* of life in a way that represents Christ is a practice that we won't always get right. We will make mistakes, ask forgiveness, and repeat the practice again and again.

Aligning yourself with the truth of God's Word is a sharpening that happens day by day. At the time I demanded that someone "do something" with my smashed suitcase, my responses from getting *bumped* in life were not exemplary.

God's justice is sure, so we can let go. We can trust that He sees, He judges rightly, and He will act in His perfect time. He calls us to live aligned with His justice—not the way of the world's compromise by taking matters into our own hands.

Just as a builder must respond wisely when something doesn't fit—adjusting the plan instead of smashing the materials—our hearts must choose release over retaliation when life's injustices crash into us. Trying to force our own justice only causes more damage. But when we surrender the situation to the Lord, He realigns what's crooked with His perfect righteousness and justice.

Reflection Questions

1. How have I responded from my flesh when I got *bumped*?

2. As I seek the Holy Spirit's direction, what is a better way to respond to that same *bump*?

3. Where have you seen or experienced injustice that was the result of a rule or law in your community, workplace, or world?

4. When the arm of the law doesn't deliver justice, are you tempted to arrange it yourself? Does that align with God's ways?

5. How does knowing that God does not partner with wicked rulers give you courage or hope?

6. In what specific ways can you align more fully with God's justice, even when the culture or systems around you do not?

7. Has someone "run over your suitcase" lately? How did you respond?

Daily Practice

Name one injustice or situation where you've been tempted to retaliate.

____

____

____

____

____

____

____

Your Turn

Write it down as a prayer of surrender, releasing it to the Lord.
Lord, I surrender......

____

____

____

____

Prayer

Lord, You see every injustice—both the ones that wound us personally and those that run deep in the world around us. Forgive me for the times I've wanted to take matters into my own hands. Help me to release retaliation and trust You fully with justice. Align my heart with Your righteousness and give me courage to live in surrender. In Jesus' name, Amen.

Threshold to Part 3

In Part 1 we named the hurt of our trauma, and in Part 2 we have moved through the mess and gained some practical wisdom, insight, and understanding of ways to process the pain. The processing of our pain has everything to do with how we heal. The pace of healing is individual. Take each day as you are able. There will be small progress for you to observe.

Think of it like a floor that needs to be replaced. When an old floor meets a new one, they don't always match. As you stand at the threshold between rooms, you may notice a difference in the height of the floors. One side needs to be built up with subflooring so that both are level. That leveling work is much like our growth through traumatic experiences—necessary to bring stability and wholeness as we step into new spaces.

As we approach Part 3, we step onto another new "floor." Often, we don't even notice the difference in the threshold because the leveling has been happening gradually. Healing is in progress—even when it's quiet.

Keep using the Emotions Wheel and "I feel" statements. Time matters. Consistency matters. One day, without realizing it, you'll notice that your healing has taken a great stride. An echo of a past situation will surface—and this time, your response will be different. You won't feel the same anxiety or turmoil you once did. That moment is evidence of God's quiet work in you. But it doesn't mean the journey is over.

In the next section, we will cover what to do when the new challenges come. And they will come. By keeping your foundation firmly rooted in Christ, you'll be equipped to face them with strength and grace.

PART 3
Rooted in Hope—Building Something New

11

Filling Rooms with Thanks

Gratefulness is what greatly expands your life to hold more joy.[16]
Ann Voskamp

In the renovation project all of the skilled workers are needed to see the job to completion. The gratitude for workers that show up at the appointed time is invaluable. Every person knows the disappointment of having a "no show" and every person knows that some situations cannot be helped. Each of us has also been the one "who didn't show." When the tile guy doesn't show up for the measurements, it is easier to overlook than when the tile guy doesn't show up on the planned installation day. The late install then makes the next step in the process have to wait. What if the tile guy lets you know ahead of time that he is not going to be able to make the designated day? This type of integrity leads to gratitude. But what do we do when this is lacking or the installer calls

---

16 Voskamp, Ann. *One Thousand Gifts: A Dare to Live Fully Right Where You Are*. Zondervan, 2010.

and says he will be delayed because the tile hasn't arrived? Disappointment happens and the tile doesn't get installed. The overall project is delayed and there is nothing we can do but accept the new revised timeline. It will also happen again on the same job. The next time may be a weather delay. We must learn to shift our focus to a better place. How do we do this? We have to train our minds to make the shift.

My Gratitude List

I distinctly recall numbering a list in 2012 while sitting in a hospital waiting room. Flint, my husband, was the patient for an exploratory heart procedure. To occupy my mind, I began writing a list of all the things I appreciate about Flint. It gave me a way of telling my mind where to go. Little did I know this practice would become a mainstay in my life. I had read Ann Voskamp's book, *One Thousand Gifts*. She teaches the reader the value of recording three gratitudes per day—little gifts from each day which she calls The Joy Dare (because who doesn't want more joy?) By the end of 365 days of practicing this, a list maker will have approximately 1,000 gifts that have been celebrated throughout the year.

Give thanks in all circumstances;
for this is the will of God in Christ Jesus for you.
1 Thessalonians 5:18

The practice began in an easy manner with Ann Voskamp's help. At the time, she would provide a calendar with a space to write and a prompt to help me "look" for the gifts. I printed it out and kept it on my refrigerator door during the day so I could jot them down as I discovered them. I recall the autumn rhythm she suggested may have gone something like this: Find three gifts eaten. Oh this is easy for me!

1. Eggs and bacon (cheating because that is two)
2. Cinnamon rolls
3. Pumpkin chocolate chip muffins

Sorry, didn't mean to make you hungry, but you get the idea. Ann Voskamp's complimentary calendars are still available on her website. They have been updated and will get you going with your own gratitudes.

In my own practice, I found that it began to transform my mind to *literally look* for the gifts during the day. Therefore, I mentally shift away from the negative and look for the good. That doesn't mean ignoring reality, but it does mean finding beauty in difficulties. These are actual gratitudes that took place during a hospital stay:

1. A kind nurse noticed that she was doing the same Bible study that I held in my hands.
2. A friend who came to visit shared the inspiration he felt while reading the book *Heaven Is for Real.*
3. Another friend brought me a favorite protein shake.

I began to notice a change in me. Although I mentally noted the "gifts" and verbalized my gratitude more frequently, my heart began a shift. I could use the gratitudes to encourage others in their own struggles. I saw the gifts at work, allowing others to feel the same joy I felt. I shared at church among our students and even taught a lesson about it in Honduras. Those orphaned children were so quick to find *ten* things each day during their week of camp. Counting it all joy made me *want* to continue the practice. People who document their gratitudes in writing enjoy the following as shared by Ann Voskamp[17]:

1. Have a relative absence of stress and depression. (Woods et al., 2008)
2. Make progress toward important personal goals. (Emmons and McCullough, 2003)
3. Report higher levels of determination and energy. (Emmons and McCullough, 2003)
4. Feel closer in their relationships and desire to build stronger relationships. (Algoe and Haidt, 2009)
5. Increase your happiness by 25 percent—who wouldn't want a quarter more happiness! (McCullough et al., 2002)

Probably the most remarkable personal benefit of practicing gratitude came through my struggle with seasonal depression. One tough January winter, the depression was so bad that my anxiety turned into speechlessness. When I was in a crowd of people, I would develop anxiety so strong I literally could not speak words. I had to get out of the crowd and allow time to pass before words would come again. For me, this was so foreign because I am a very chatty, outgoing person.

Imagine my relief and *joy* at not having seasonal depression any longer! I moved the practice of writing gratitudes from the refrigerator door to my journal. Each day, I write and number them. The next day, I pick up with the next number so that at any time I know how many "gifts" or gratitudes I have written for the year. As of this morning, I have 1,536 for the current

---

17 Voskamp, Ann. "Take the Joy Dare." *AnnVoskamp.com*, Ann Voskamp, October 2025, https://annvoskamp.com/joy-dares/.

year. Obviously I write more than three a day, but some days I have written zero, although it is the exception to miss a day or two.

When a day or season is particularly hard, I intentionally write more! Usually I write them in the mornings, but I have written them at all times of the day. I carry my journal with me when I anticipate unoccupied wait times like hospitals and doctor's offices particularly. Gratitudes have become a lifeline for me, keeping me grounded in all the good things that are happening even in the midst of hard seasons. I continually catch myself looking for all the good things. This is not to minimize that difficulties are happening, but it does help my mind to dwell where it should.

> Finally, brothers, whatever is true,
> whatever is honorable, whatever is just,
> whatever is pure, whatever is lovely,
> whatever is commendable, if there is any excellence,
> if there is anything worthy of praise,
> think about these things.
> Philippians 4:8

As we think of all the workers on the house renovation who help bring a job to completion, there is abundant gratitude. Their skills have been honed over decades, and they may even be using the opportunities to train up others in their craft. They show up with integrity at the appointed time with effort for the needed tasks, or they give appropriate notifications so adjustments can be made in the overall project.

Our lives are like that. In order to present ourselves to Christ, we must show up. In seasons of difficulty like you are enduring, showing up is difficult. Little steps, just three gratitudes a day, can help you to function in the present moment. Your thoughts can be focused; you can reflect on the gratitude you have recently experienced and appreciate the many small gifts in your life. By doing this, you are showing up for *yourself.* Yes, it can be beneficial to your family relationships, but the main person it helps is YOU. You are present in the current moment and your intentions are set on continuing the practice because you *want* to do it.

Reflection Questions

1. What are the first gratitudes that come to your mind naturally?

2. Do you prefer a guided calendar for your refrigerator to write 3 gifts daily or will you write them in your own journal? (See the resources for Ann Voskamp's latest templates)

3. In a renovation project, gratitude is shown when workers arrive with integrity and complete their part. Who in your life has "shown up" for you in a way that sparked gratitude?

Daily Practice

I enjoy numerical sequencing because it provides a sense of accomplishment and is built-in accountability. If my numerical count has not increased, it is easy for me to identify and correct that! Choose the method that is a good fit for you. That will help you build upon this mind- and life-changing habit.

It is helpful to me to encourage others to use this method of writing gratitudes. I often read a few of them in my small group or one-on-one with a friend who has confessed their struggle with depression, negative thinking, or anxiety. I have texted them to others, shared via social media, and I always end the year with a social post about what this has done to transform my life since 2011. Many people have reported back to me their success in using this helpful daily rhythm and the impact in their own lives.

Your Turn

Take a few quiet minutes writing here or in your journal. For each prompt, write down one gift from today. Don't overthink it—let the first things that come to mind flow onto the page.

- Something you saw today that made you smile

- Something you heard that encouraged you

- Something you tasted or smelled that brought comfort

- Someone who "showed up" for you in a small or big way

- A way you sensed God's presence, even if subtle

Maybe you are thankful for *things* like air conditioning in the summer. I notice that it shows up 3 or 4 times in my gratitudes during the summer months. Or you might be thankful *for things* like an ingredient to a recipe that you didn't expect to find in your pantry. The gifts also arrive with thankfulness in *things* like a song that comforts you while you're grieving a loss or a beautiful sunrise to bring a smile on a hard morning.

After you write a few, pause and read them slowly. It doesn't minimize sad circumstances; it acknowledges the good among them. It helps us with a way to cope with difficulties everyday.

Prayer

Lord, thank You for these gifts. Train my heart to keep seeing Your goodness, even here. Thank You for being Lord over all of my life. Your sovereignty reigns over me and my life in every single way. You make every move of the weather and You use it for Your glory. Allow me to accept the mystery of all that You are and all that You accomplish. Forgive me for my failures. Forgive me for not seeing all the places where You are at work. Help me to continually confess my failures to You and walk in the freedom of Your forgiveness. Thank You for Your truth in thanksgiving and directing me to give thanks in all circumstances and for all things. Let my gratitude continually be a praise offering to You. May I be transformed into Your image a little more every single day. In Jesus' name I pray. Amen.

12

Practices to Reinforce Our Foundation

Imagine yourself as a living house. God comes in to rebuild that house.
At first, perhaps, you can understand what He is doing...
But presently He starts knocking the house about
in a way that hurts abominably and does not seem to make sense.
You thought you were going to be made into
a decent little cottage: but He is building a palace.[18]
C.S. Lewis

On the surface, a house can look beautiful—fresh paint, clean lines, everything in its place. But when the inspector arrives and starts looking closer, hidden problems can emerge: wood rot behind the siding, foundation cracks spreading slowly, a roof that's been leaking unnoticed for years, or lack of pest prevention taking its toll in the crawlspace. I've seen homes that passed a buyer's approval when viewed thoroughly via photos, but had serious issues

---

18 Lewis, C.S. *Mere Christianity*. HarperOne, 1952.

when seeing in person because no one had cared for it over time. Regular maintenance had been ignored, and what was once strong began to quietly break down.

Our spiritual lives can be the same. We might appear steady on the outside, but if we neglect consistent practices like reading the Bible, prayer, worship, and gathering with other believers, the unseen structure of our faith can weaken. The deterioration is often slow and silent, but over time, the lack of consistent spiritual practice shows. Faithfulness in these rhythms isn't for keeping up appearances—it reinforces the interior structure of our lives so that when the storms come, we can stand firm.

> One who is faithful in a very little is also faithful in much, and one who is dishonest in a very little is also dishonest in much. If then you have not been faithful in the unrighteous wealth, who will entrust to you the true riches?
> Luke 16:10–11

Daily Discipleship

In the years I taught middle and high school students at our church, I saw the daily practices of Bible reading and prayer help the students grow in remarkable ways. When they didn't understand a passage, I taught them to dig deeper with dictionaries and concordances. Still they often said, "But I don't understand."

In those moments, I would point them to Luke 16:10–11 and remind them that our responsibility is to live according to the parts of scripture we *do* understand. If we faithfully apply what we already know, God will honor that obedience by entrusting us with "true riches"—deeper insight and greater understanding of His Word.

Every Bible reading plan will include Scripture that puzzles us. For example, in my own personal reading today from Leviticus, I understood the concepts, but they came from a broader, elevated view. To see the Lord's design for rhythms of rest, reliance, freedom, and stewardship, I needed to connect it with other parts of Scripture.

That's why Luke's words resonate so deeply: Not every reading produces a single "aha" verse for immediate application. Sometimes the takeaway is found in themes that unfold over many passages.

I share this to remind you that even those who have studied the Bible for decades don't have banner days every time they read. The key is faithfulness. We stay in the Word, apply what we understand, and pray for the Holy Spirit to reveal more as we grow.

As we desire to be accountable to the Lord and others, one little trick has helped me immensely: keeping a "streak." I learned this during youth ministry, and I am unsure if a student shared the idea or another ministry partner shared it: Keep a number of your days.

Each time when you sit down to be with the Lord, number the day. This year, I had worked my way up to 129 days in a row and would just jot the number at the top of the journal pages for the day. Certainly I could see the fruit from my consistency and had also paired this practice with refraining from using my phone until after my quiet time was complete. I had more peace, clarity, joy, and gratitude than I could have imagined possible. It's amazing what putting your phone down will do!

Then one week, I was reading a terrific book about the Holy Spirit. I finished it in the early morning with tears in my eyes.

I had another obligation right after that and my day began. It was a great day, but the next morning I opened my journal to discover I had missed reading and journaling so I had to start my streak all over again. *At number one*. Yikes. I shared the agony with a friend who knew the exact feeling as she is building her streak too.

Being consistent in the practices that fuel my faith are important to me because I know they make a difference. I am most prepared for any circumstance when I have surrendered to the Lord through prayer, confessed my sin to Him, meditated upon His Word, and looked for life application. And of course, I thank Him for all that He is doing and desire to be attentive to join Him in His work.

A former student leader, River, kept track of his Bible reading and prayer "streak" on a whiteboard in his room. The number had climbed impressively high, and he was proud to share it with the youth group. One day, his younger brother, Sawyer, decided to *erase* River's record of his streak. Missing a single day of reading or prayer wasn't really the issue, but that moment stuck with Sawyer. Even now, he remembers it. The point is never perfection; it is about staying faithful and keeping the process going in order to *continually connect with the Lord*.

When I reached out to River to see if he recalled the number of his streak, he said, "I had approximately four years of consecutive daily reading when I decided that the number had become more important to me than what I was reading. At that point I stopped counting and haven't kept a streak since. Of course, there isn't anything wrong with doing it as long as it serves to motivate and doesn't become the master."

It isn't the streak that matters, but the accountability of it mentally helps us to continue the habit over days, weeks, months, years, and soon it will be decades, and your transformation will be so dramatic you will wonder how you ever lived without the Word of God every single day.

Just like a house that looks beautiful from the outside can quietly deteriorate without regular maintenance, our spiritual lives require faithful attention over time. Reading the Bible, gathering with believers, praying, and worshipping are habits for faith fueling. By tending to these practices faithfully, we aren't just keeping up appearances; we're preserving the integrity of what God has built in us, reinforcing the structure to withstand both time and storms.

Reflection Questions

1. What daily or weekly practices keep your spiritual structure strong?

2. In what areas of your faith life do you tend to "defer maintenance"?

3. Which small habits (reading, gathering, prayer) have strengthened you most over time?

4. How does consistency in spiritual disciplines shape how you handle life's storms?

Daily Practice

Simply add a number to your days of journaling to help you build consistency. Follow River's advice and don't let the number become more important than what you are reading!

Your Turn

Take a moment to reflect on your current spiritual practices. Which habits are strong, and which might need some "maintenance"? Write down one practical step you'll take this week to strengthen your daily or weekly rhythm—whether it's Bible reading, setting aside prayer time, or re-engaging with your church community.

____

____

____

____

Prayer

Lord, You have given us one another along with Your Word as a model for how we are to be working out our salvation day by day. Forgive me when I am in a worldly hurry. Help me to not be in a hurry when it comes to You. Help me linger in your presence. Thank You for Your compassion and Your heart for Your people. Allow the Holy Spirit to grant us the opportunity to know You more deeply and have the discipline to seek You first everyday. I love You, Lord. In Jesus' name I pray. Amen.

13

Refreshing Others

*Those who are happiest are those who
do the most for others.*[19]
Booker T. Washington

The construction site is one of the clearest pictures of this principle at work: Each trade lifts the whole structure by doing its part faithfully. They aren't necessarily always working together, but their connection with the builder helps them all to know and have the shared goal of completing their part to the established expectations and to do it in a specific time frame. In the same way, as followers of Christ, we may not all know one another personally, but we submit to the same Heavenly Father and work toward His purposes.

It's so sweet when you meet a stranger, like what happened at the local bookstore on Friday: Samara heard my daughter and me talking about the need for paper towels in the restroom

---

19 Washington, Booker T. *Up from Slavery*. Doubleday, Page & Co., 1901.

and popped her head around the corner to let us know she had taken care of that issue. I thought it was kind of her to let us know. Later, I introduced myself to her and learned about her new adventures living in America for only about six weeks. Our conversation turned to the book I am writing, which opened the door to her broad beautiful smile as she exclaimed, "Oh, you're a Christian! I am a Christian too." I was so happy for the instant connection as we walked together to look at a book that had caught my eye earlier.

It's that instant connection many times when we meet a fellow believer, and I felt that way about meeting Samara. We may only know one another briefly from the bookstore, but we know we both submit to the same Heavenly Father, and therefore have lots of other things in common. One of the things that believers have in common is caring for one another. Even a small encounter like that can be life-giving—a reminder that God refreshes us through the unexpected kindness of His people.

That's why so many people express love through food—by baking a cake, cooking a meal, or setting a welcoming table. God uses the gifts He's given us for His glory. When people are hurting, they still need nourishing food and a bit of kindness. Sharing a meal around a table brings comfort to both the giver and the receiver.

Sometimes the most simple way to refresh another person is with a handwritten note. In a world of quick texts and scrolling messages, a few thoughtful lines on paper can carry lasting weight. A note says, *"I see you. I remember you. You matter to me."* Whether it's a verse of Scripture, a word of thanks, or a reminder of God's faithfulness, written encouragement has a way of lingering, long after the envelope is opened. It becomes a tangible expression of love—a small offering that can lift a weary heart and remind someone that they're not walking alone.

On a cold winter morning, I was volunteering by phone for a prayer ministry, answering calls and praying with the callers. My first caller was from a person who was negative, complaining, and wanted to tell me exactly how to pray for him because the last volunteer had not done it correctly from his point of view. All of this is perfectly fine, but he could not stop complaining long enough so that I could actually pray with him. Finally, he allowed me to pray and the call ended.

The very next caller had a bright and cheerful, "This is Veronica, and I called to pray *for you!*" She went on to explain that she was financially broken with no computer, so she could not serve as a volunteer. However, she was able to call in to pray for the volunteers answering the calls *so that we would be encouraged by her prayers*. And the timing was perfect. I needed her encouragement at that exact moment. We never know how God is going to use refreshment whether we are the giver or the receiver. His timing and delivery are perfect.

After Matthew's survival of the cardiac arrest, I felt a deep desire to help others just as we had been helped. I realized that our church didn't even have one AED; now we have three. That led me to think about the unknowns of using the AED or the necessary responses if an AED is unavailable. I began organizing CPR certification classes in our community. Certified instructors partnered with our church, united by a shared faith in the same Heavenly Father. The instructors volunteered their time and the church offered its space freely. My role was to spread the word and invite anyone who wanted to learn. Together, we celebrated the miracle of survivorship and the power of simple, quick actions that save lives.

This effort also increased awareness in our community—at churches, ballfields, and gathering places—about the need for AED equipment so that CPR could be performed anywhere people meet. Watching the awareness spread is life-giving. It deeply encouraged me to see so many people become certified and ready to save a life. I was witnessing it firsthand: *healing people heal people.*

> Whoever brings blessing will be enriched,
> and one who waters will himself be watered.
> Proverbs 11:25

This verse beautifully captures what we can experience through each of those simple, ordinary moments—the conversation at the bookstore, the giving of food, the handwritten notes of encouragement, and organizing the CPR classes. Every act of service—whether it is teaching life-saving skills, preparing a meal, or speaking a kind word—becomes a way to pour into others. And in God's goodness, He uses those same moments to pour refreshment back into our own hearts. The truth of Proverbs 11:25 came alive before my eyes: When we water others through love and obedience, the Living Water flows right back to us. Just as water refreshes us, nourishing and sustaining us from within, God's Spirit moves through His people, strengthening the body of Christ.

Refreshing others isn't limited to those who already know Jesus. Each day offers us the chance to pour into others through kindness, prayer, or simple presence. And we trust the outcome to God. On a job site, not every worker knows the builder by name, yet each one's effort contributes to the beauty and strength of the finished home. When we listen to the Master Builder's voice and follow His plans, we become like living water running through the pipes of His house. This flows from room to room, bringing renewal wherever it goes. Under His steady hand, the framework of faith is strengthened. What once was merely construction now becomes a dwelling filled with life, light, and refreshment.

Reflection Questions

1. What times can you recall that you have been refreshed by others?

2. What about times where you have been the one refreshing another?

3. What relational healing have you witnessed in either of these cases?

4. Who might God be calling you to refresh in this season?

Daily Practice

Look for one small way to refresh someone today—through a word of encouragement, a practical act of service, or praying with them. It doesn't have to be big; small acts of kindness ripple widely when done under the Builder's direction. Jot down what that might be.

Your Turn

Take a moment to write about one way God has used someone to refresh you—and one way you could use your gifts to refresh someone else this week.

____

____

____

____

____

____

____

Prayer

Lord, thank You for Your sovereignty and the people You've placed in my life to refresh and encourage me. Forgive me when I have missed opportunities to refresh others or have not noticed when someone was trying to refresh me. Give me eyes to notice where You provide openings for me to refresh others with kindness, service, and words that bring life. Keep my eyes on You, the Builder, so that all I do points back to You for Your glory. May my life be a source of blessing, just as You continually refresh me. In Jesus' name, Amen.

14

Reframing Our Thoughts

*Your life is always moving in the
direction of your strongest thoughts.*[20]
Craig Groeschel

On a building site, the weather can't be controlled, but preparation can. As a seasoned builder, Flint has trained himself to monitor weather patterns. I fondly refer to my dear hubby as "the weatherman." I wake up to "better have your rain jacket today" or "it's going to be a cold one" and "I've gotta go out to Long Run Farm and cover those bricks before the rain comes." When any weather system is coming, he's out there covering materials and checking the site, even at odd hours. Over time, this mindset has become second nature to him. In the same way, our thought life must be intentionally trained. We can't control the weather systems that bring a storm, but we can prepare, protect, and reframe what we face through a renewed mind.

---

20 Groeschel, Craig. *Winning the War in Your Mind: Change Your Thinking, Change Your Life.* Zondervan, 2021.

And take every thought captive to obey Christ.
2 Corinthians 10:5b

Reframing Tragedy

In 2023, at the end of our family vacation, we decided to pack up on Friday night to be ready to leave early on Saturday morning. We are morning people, but this has never been a vacation practice to leave for home in the early morning. Our son Matthew & his wife, Elizabeth, had left early for a friend's wedding. Our daughter and son-in-law were packing up to leave early so their baby could sleep on the ride home.

Flint and I were awakened that Saturday morning at 5 a.m. with a call from our neighbor asking if we were okay, as there was an emergency happening at our home. We had a house sitter so we immediately started praying for those involved and their families. We jumped into our clothes, got into the loaded car, and started the three-hour drive home. You might imagine all the thoughts going through our heads on the drive home. We both knew we couldn't let our thoughts run wild, so we prayed, asking God to take our thoughts captive and make them obedient to Him.

Years later as Carson Furr, our house sitter at the time, and I reflected on the happenings that day, Carson said it had been a good week. He and his friend Dalton Gay had been preparing all week for the Saturday morning training of FCA student leaders. They were also planning a future evangelistic outreach for students and were dreaming of who could speak, hopefully Grant Ketron. Where would the event be hosted? What steps were needed to get the most possible students there so that they could hear about Jesus? Together they identified many of these details. At the moment, they only knew they were making plans. Unknown to them, the Lord was establishing their steps for what was about to occur.

The heart of man plans his way,
but the LORD establishes his steps.
Proverbs 16:9

Because Carson and Dalton knew Flint and I would be home on Saturday, they had our home all ready for us. On Friday night, they had laid out their clothing and supplies for the FCA meeting on the kitchen table. They could grab their things and leave quickly Saturday morning. In hindsight, Carson believes the Lord had all the details in order because "coincidental" happenings are not without the finger of God.

They both went to sleep on Friday with plans in their heads and excitement for the FCA training the next day. Carson woke up in the early morning on Saturday realizing Dalton needed help and immediately called 911. Carson recalled noises from a seizure and Dalton's unconscious state. He followed the instructions of the 911 operator and help arrived quickly. It is nearly unbelievable: Dalton passed away from cardiac arrest at our home.

Flint and I both knew this was no coincidence that we are praying for another family affected by cardiac arrest. We did not know Dalton but only knew that he was Carson's friend. Why would God choose our home? We knew if Dalton's death occurred at Dalton's home or in another setting, it could cause trauma for a greater number of people close to him. Why this timing, at the end of our vacation? (A selfish, yet honest question.) We knew we were more rested and better equipped to handle a tragedy after vacation than we would be at any other time. We verbalized this to one another and experienced the peaceful feeling to think that *God had chosen our home* for this. We were consciously reframing our thoughts.

Reframing requires beliefs, assumptions, and values to be examined. We must mentally bring our thoughts into alignment with our values. And our values align with our belief in His Word.

People ask, "Why is this happening *to* me?" Reframe your thoughts and consider this: "This is happening *for* me."

Why would this happening *for* us be of any value? We have experience in this, and God can use us to encourage Carson and his family.

What good can possibly come from this? Our responses to the situation can fuel the faith of others.

In recollection of this series of events, Carson notes many provisions from the Lord: four firefighters he knew who provided familiarity. The responding officer was the dad of Carson's friend from high school—he had a very calming presence, steady demeanor, and asked helpful questions.

Carson called Dalton's mother to tell her the heart-wrenching news that Dalton had died. He walked toward the kitchen as he spoke to her. The "Jesus Won" t-shirt they had laid out the night before caught his eye, and the Holy Spirit came over him with the thoughts of making a choice to only be ALL IN for Jesus.

Carson had already made the choice to surrender his life to Jesus long before this day, but he surrendered again as he faced the loss of his best friend. With that surrender, total peace came over him. *Everything will be okay.* Even with the loss of Dalton's life and the unimaginable grief of Dalton's mother, Carson knew everything would be okay because of Jesus.

This is peace that surpasses all understanding as referred to in Philippians 4:7.

The evangelistic student outreach Carson and Dalton had planned was to be held weeks in the future. Yet from Carson's point of view, it unfolded in the hours of that worst day and the next day, the best day. Carson shared the *sad news* of Dalton's passing with friends (the very students he spent many hours discipling) AND the *good news* of Jesus Christ. He made a conscious decision to view the events through a certain lens, looking for all the parallels between what he and Dalton had planned for the evangelistic outreach and the celebration of Dalton's life as it unfolded. Carson reframed his thoughts too!

The following day, Sunday, the best day, was led by the very pastor they wanted for their evangelistic student out-reach plans, Grant Ketron. You see, Grant was not the usual pastor to be preaching on Sunday morning at their church. He was filling in for the pastor who was away on an inter-national mission trip. At the worship services, with a great number of students and family members present, Dalton's grandmother gave her life to Christ among many others who did so that day.

On Sunday night, the theater of Carson High School was so filled with students there was standing room only. The most possible students they could reach were present. Carson, helped by the Holy Spirit, spoke at the very end of the night. Carson had peace knowing God was using these things for His glory.

> And we know that for those who love God
> all things work together for good, for those
> who are called according to his purpose.
> Romans 8:28

As an FCA Leader, Dalton had shared in a testimonial video earlier in 2023. "Through the Lord, my life has been transformed to be something better, to live for something more than just myself. The Lord has given me the ability to have eternal life with him." You can watch the entire video of Dalton's testimony link in the Resources.

The Lord wants to reframe your story: What if this is happening *for you,* not *to you*? We immediately knew that God had chosen our home for this. We knew the potential situations that could have occurred for Dalton's family, and the Lord saw fit to *choose our home* and Carson's presence rather than another setting. Our first response was to pray for this young man that we did not know but shared a kinship because of Carson and the family of God. We prayed for his family and we called on our warriors to pray with us for Dalton, his family, and for all aspects of this situation. The resilience God gives us does not make any of us immune to human feelings, but He allows us to continually put our faith in Him. We trust Him because He knows what is best.

Reframing our thoughts comes through practicing the acts of surrender, which moves us from dwelling on our own solution and releasing it to the Lord for His solution instead. Viewing our lives from a point of gratitude and counting the gifts daily is another reframing. Instead of being sad because there is a rainy day, we look for ways we might receive rest instead. The more we practice reframing, the more we will automatically begin to do it. When we seek scripture and prayer daily, the Holy Spirit transforms our minds, and reframing is a part of that.

As you await His details unfolding in your life, may you find His comfort in songs that have comforted me. See the Resources for a helpful playlist link.

Like a builder who checks the forecast and prepares the site, we can't control the storms, but we can guard our minds. Allowing God to train our thoughts to rest on His character and promises prepares us to stand firm in every storm.

Reflection Questions

1. What "weather patterns" / warnings in your thought life need your attention right now?

2. Where have you seen God reframe painful circumstances into something meaningful over time?

3. Which Scriptures or truths help you reframe your thoughts when unexpected storms come?

4. Is there a situation you need to surrender to God's reframing today?

Daily Practice

Take a situation that feels overwhelming or discouraging and *intentionally reframe it* by writing out one or several of God's promises over it (e.g., Romans 8:28; Proverbs 16:9; Isaiah 55:8–9). Say it aloud, pray it through, and choose to trust His greater plan.

Example: The situation is a new diagnosis for a friend, "Karen's," illness. Lord, thank You for Karen's life. I know that You love Karen and want to work all things for her good. Karen is called according to Your purposes. Help her to see Your purposes in this diagnosis. I want to help her in this journey. We have plans, but help us to surrender our plans to You and Your will. I want to allow You to order my steps just for today, in love, for Karen. Bring to my mind what I need in the moment I need it. Conform my thoughts to Your thoughts and my ways to Your ways. In Jesus' name I pray. Amen.

Now pick one of the verses and write it here:

Your Turn

Write down one situation where your thoughts have been running wild. Ask the Lord to help you see it through His perspective. Write out your prayer if that helps, using the verse you chose. What new lens might God be giving you? Be patient with yourself. Transformation takes time.

Prayer

Lord, thank You that You are the Master Builder who sees the full forecast. You are all knowing of every detail that has happened and will happen. Train my mind to rest on the truth of Your Word. You are our Comforter and know my grief. Forgive me when I lose sight of that. Reframe my thoughts when fear, confusion or sorrow rise. Help me trust that You are working all things together for good, even when I cannot see it. Renew my mind daily, and give me eyes to recognize Your hand in every story. In Jesus' name. Amen.

15

Redeeming All Things

There is not a square inch in the whole domain of our human existence over which Christ, who is Sovereign over all, does not cry: "Mine!"[21]
Abraham Kuyper

When the final touches are complete on a renovation, there's a moment when the house is ready to be lived in again. Walls once cracked are now sturdy. Windows that leaked now let in the light. The floorboards don't creak; they sing. But the true beauty of the home isn't found in the paint or the fixtures—it's in its purpose being restored. A home is meant to be inhabited, to shelter life, and welcome others. In the same way, God doesn't just patch the broken places in our lives; He redeems them, weaving them into His greater story in just the right timing that He chooses. The house stands not only strong, but radiant, testifying to the skill of the Master Builder.

---

21 Kuyper, Abraham. "Sphere Sovereignty." *Inaugural Address*, Free University of Amsterdam, 1880.

He has made everything beautiful in its time.
Also, he has put eternity into man's heart,
yet so that he cannot find out what God has done
from the beginning to the end.
Ecclesiastes 3:11

We don't get to choose which stories are redeemed here on earth and which ones are redeemed in heaven. When I look for His hand and His timing, I notice the large and small gifts that are only noticeable if we are paying full attention.

One of God's greatest stories is the way He answers prayers when parents pray for their children's future spouses. We prayed for the spouses of our children from an early age. Specifically, we prayed that their spouses would be raised in godly homes by Christian parents who valued marriage. We also prayed prayers that our children put on a list themselves when they were old enough. Our son-in-law has blue eyes, just like our daughter prayed for. Our children's spouses far exceed all we could hope for in bonus children. That is just like God to do that!

Does God have your full attention? Are you faithfully bringing all your requests to Him as you talk with Him each day? All our requests are important to Him. Not just our worries, but our celebrations too.

Delight yourselves in the LORD, and
he will give you the desires of your heart.
Psalm 37:4

Redeeming a Date

One of our delights was when our son Matthew became engaged to Elizabeth in June of 2022. We were having a conversation that night between Elizabeth, her mother, and me about the possibilities of their wedding being the same year. They told me that her brother, a college athlete, would only be available one date in December of 2022. *December 17*. At that moment, I asked Elizabeth if she knew the significance of the date, December 17. She knew it was her parents' wedding anniversary, but she did not know it was the date that Matthew had survived cardiac arrest.

Elizabeth had always wanted to get married at a historical inn in downtown Anderson, South Carolina. Her mother called the inn on the following Monday and learned *they had a cancellation.* Only one date was available: for none other than *December 17!*

Isn't that just like God to take something seemingly small to some, that anniversary of cardiac arrest, and make it brand new? I always had a big lump in my throat in the late fall season. It colored the holidays for Flint and me. The beginning of wrestling season would remind me of the days of taking Matthew to school early for Driver's Education and not seeing him again until the end of the evening when wrestling was over. Our high school hosted an annual wrestling tournament. Matthew had a challenging match at the tournament that weekend and sat with our athletic trainer for a while afterward just a few days before his cardiac arrest. None of us knew what was coming, but the Lord did.

As those dates would roll around on the calendar, hearing discussions of wrestling matches would bring back memories. In the early years since then, we pressed forward in the Lord's strength to attend quite a few matches to watch our nephew eventually win the state title in his weight class. It was a big celebration in Greensboro, North Carolina, and I often enjoy watching the video replay of his big win. In the highs and lows of life, the remembrances causing our anxiety were still there.

Jeremiah 32 holds one of the many examples in the Word of God demonstrating His absolute power. Jeremiah had been praying for understanding, acknowledging God's power and the disaster that had come among the disobedient people. He is confused about being told to purchase a field even though the city is about to be overtaken.

Behold, I am the LORD, the God of all flesh.
Is anything too hard for me?
Jeremiah 32:27

God gives the city over to those who are fighting against them *along with a promise* that he will gather His people back to the same place and allow them to dwell in safety.

And they shall be my people, and I will be their God.
Jeremiah 32:38

He is keeping His promises to His people. He is demonstrating that He has done it then, and we know that He will do it again in our own lives. I have seen Him redeem time. He literally has made ordinary tasks of the day go much quicker than expected after I have invested hours praying with others. I have seen redeemed marriages with a healthy one after abuse caused the first one to fail. He redeems lives. This even shows up in popular Christian songs when beautiful lyrics emerge from an endured struggle. Our struggles are not wrapped up with a happy ending in a pretty song, but God does encourage us to show us that He is present and that He is redeeming some things now and some things will wait.

For us, a new marriage, a new beginning, and a beautiful addition of Elizabeth to our family is more than we ever hoped and dreamed. All of these were given to us to celebrate that date, December 17. No more anticipation during the fall season of that dreaded date. We have been freed from that. God can do anything. He can even redeem a date! That is worthy of celebration.

As I look back over the dozen years that have passed since Matthew's *survival* of cardiac arrest, I see God's leadership of our lives. Our activated faith has allowed us to walk in obedience. Some people experience *joyful* obedience. We are ordinary people, not always joyful and not even always obedient. Yet we are being perfected a little each day by our Creator.

The anxiety and trauma has been redeemed in numerous ways:

- Seeing His power and witnessing to others about it.
- Choosing faith over fear as we release our children and their children to the Lord again and again in each new life stage.
- Being courageous to process our pain over many years.
- Developing a fruitful relationship with our counselor.
- Allowing transparency of our lives to encourage others.
- Operating from a place of rest.
- Accepting the Lord's plans for our lives whether or not we consider it "fair".
- Faithfully worshipping and seeking community with our church family.
- Submitting our lives to the transformation provided through His Word and prayer.

The renovated house is nearly complete, yet the family inside is what makes it a home. But even more than that, it carries a story—of storms weathered, foundations reinforced, and rooms filled with joy. In God's hands, the test becomes a testimony. He redeems it all. Some of that has taken place already, some is about to take place, and some of that will take place when we meet Jesus face-to-face in heaven.

Reflection Questions

1. Where have you seen God bring redemption out of something broken in someone's life?

2. What situations or relationships in your life are in need of restoration?

3. What might help you to trust in His timing?

4. How might your "rebuilt house" be used to bless and shelter others?

Daily Practice

Take time to list specific situations, hurts, or seasons where you've witnessed God's redemption—even in small ways. Thank Him for each one. Then list areas still in process and pray over them, surrendering them to His timing.

____

____

____

____

____

____

Your Turn

Write a "before and after" reflection on a specific area of your life that God has redeemed—or one you're trusting Him to redeem. What do you see now that you couldn't see before?

____

____

____

____

____

Prayer

Lord, thank You that You are the Redeemer of all things. Thank You for taking what the enemy meant for harm and turning it into good. Forgive me when I become impatient or frustrated as I wait. Help me to trust You in the places that are still being redeemed. May my days, like a restored home, shine as a testimony to Your goodness, welcoming others into Your story. In Jesus' name, Amen.

Summary:
Reflection & Renewal

Eleven months ago, while Dianne and I walked along the beach, the Lord gave me the vision for this metaphor of the house and the way to use it in the book. I didn't yet know how He would weave it all together, but I trusted that He would. I know when the Lord delivers a message, He does so completely. I just needed to wait for His timing, and of course, it is true again in this setting. It is true in your setting too. He won't fail us. He won't.

Friend, I am so proud of you for having completed your first pass through a redemptive journey. This has been a guided walk through the trauma toward the beauty of a God-centered life that is being rebuilt. Take a moment to celebrate what you have accomplished, walking through something sacred.

I want to acknowledge the pain and the despair that you have likely felt in varying degrees till all hours. My hope is that you have taken the considerable amount of time that was needed to examine all of it. The cracks, facing the mess, and trusting the Master Builder to redeem every part of your story. With compassion, I want you to know that you will not regret the investment of time needed for healing, and only the Lord knows the time frame for you. Continually pursuing Him, you can revisit the practices and slowly develop your daily rhythms to process everything life has brought and what it will bring in the future. Let's revisit your accomplishments so far.

Part 1: Naming What Hurts—Understanding the Wound

Your hurts have been documented through your written reflections. You will get better at identifying those each day so that you can continually learn to recognize what causes certain emotions to arise. You are not alone. There are so many others experiencing similar pain. Through Scripture and gentle reflection, naming your pain and fears honestly and laying them before God, the One who already knows every broken place, brings freedom. The relief that you have felt so far is just the beginning, and there is more freedom ahead as you come to know yourself and your Maker more completely. This is the foundation of all healing: honesty before a God who already knows and loves you.

Part 2: Moving Through the Mess—Ways to Process the Pain

Like a renovation site mid-project, our healing can look chaotic. You've slowed down to explore the practices of surrender, noticing gifts every day, and seeking godly community. These are practical tools for steadying the soul in the midst of disruption. The biblical wisdom and shared personal experiences help you to process trauma through the lens of your faith in Christ. What shifts have you noticed? You no longer *have* to do this; you *get* to. This daily surrender is a reframing in itself. Which of these rhythms has become most life-giving for you?

Part 3: Rooted in Hope—Building Something New

Your healing doesn't end with repair; it blossoms into redemption. In this final section, we looked to God's redemptive power to redeem all things. He redeems relationships, memories, dates on the calendar, even the unseen corners of your heart. I encourage you to continue pursuing the "transformed house" with a deep trust in the Master Builder. Not every part of our stories has been fully redeemed yet—mine included. But God's redemptive work is ongoing. As you continue building, your life becomes a testimony, one that can shelter and inspire others.

In the end, *Firm Foundation: Resilience After Trauma* reminds you that no matter how fierce the storm or deep the cracks, **God is the Builder who makes all things new**. May He encourage you so much through this that you become able to encourage someone else who would also like to build resilience after trauma.

> Blessed be the God and Father of our Lord Jesus Christ,
> the Father of mercies and God of all comfort,
> who comforts us in all our affliction,
> so that we may be able to comfort
> those who are in any affliction, with the comfort
> with which we ourselves are comforted by God.
> 2 Corinthians 1:3–4

If God has provided hope and a new perception of your trauma through this book, consider telling a friend. I believe the act of refreshing others is part of our healing, which is why I have testified many times to what He has done and is doing. Consider gifting a copy of this book to a friend. May your rebuilt life stand as a beacon of hope, drawing others toward the Master Builder. As you move forward, may the lyrics of "Firm Foundation" by Cody Carnes become your anthem. See the Resources for the link.

Your story is not over. In fact, it's being rebuilt on the Firm Foundation that cannot be shaken. Keep walking with the Master Builder—He won't fail you. He won't.

150

Resources:

Salvation through Jesus Christ
https://peacewithgod.net

Video Testimony of Dalton Gay
https://youtu.be/nlLhMKWqrcI

American Association of Christian Counselors
christiancareconnect.com

Playlist on Spotify

Storyworth
https://www.storyworth.com/

Daily Devotion Recommendations:

Experiencing God Day by Day
https://a.co/d/03jHQQJq

Experiencing God Day by Day Podcast
https://experiencinggoddaybydaypodcast.libsyn.com

Seeing Jesus Together
https://www.seeingjesustogether.com/

Pause App
https://wildatheart.org/apps/one-minute-pause/